The Alchemy Spoon
Issue 11

The Alchemy Spoon
Issue 11

A poetry magazine with a special interest in 'new phase' poets

Design and production
Clayhanger Press

Typeset in Times New Roman

Poetry Submissions
Our submission window is next open from 1 – 29 February 2024
The theme for the issue is 'Elements'

Please read the submissions guidelines on the final page
Submissions are through the website
www.alchemyspoon.org

Cover Images

Front Cover: *Coloured Pencils, Barolo, Italy*, photograph by Roger Camp
Back Cover: *Colour Research 1*, oil on board by Jasper Deane

ISSN 2365-0513
ISBN 978-1-7391770-9-6

I prefer living in colour.
David Hockney

Contents

Editorial

Colour! What a deep and mysterious language,
the language of dreams.
(Paul Gauguin)[1]

It was at the launch of Issue 10 of *The Alchemy Spoon* where, after being introduced as guest editor with a fondness for Malbec, I threw down the gauntlet and invited poets to respond to the theme of 'colours'. I brandished prompts, like responding to Ted Hughes's poem, *Red* about Sylvia Plath[2], by thinking about colours associated with a particular person. I also dwelt indulgently on my time in Japan, citing expressions with colour embedded in them, such as *aka chan* (baby), literally 'little red thing', and *aka no tannin* (complete stranger), literally 'red stranger', and suggested considering colours in the context of another culture.

I secretly congratulated myself on a broad theme that might elicit wide-ranging responses and was pleased by the hundreds of poems we received. However, reading through interpretations of the theme, I came to realise that it is one thing to write about colours, and quite another thing to avoid doing so in a contrived manner. Or, perhaps after intensive research, to resist the temptation to lean in to a 'colour inventory'. I thought back to my own lacklustre attempts to write on colour in MA workshops and grasped the difficulty of coming at the task 'through the back window' as a brilliant poet once said to me.

Nevertheless, many rose to the challenge, and the subjects of the poems in this issue range from artists and paintings to illness, grief, abuse, nature, love, and poems rooted in place, such as 'The Baltic Flour Mill', 'Salary Man' (the Japanese loan word for businessman) and 'Peploe in Cassis'. Not surprisingly, given my own connections to Japan, I found that L B Jørgensen's evocation of a Japanese job 'won in a blue-clad interview' and of office workers on the train whose bodies are 'sea anemones swaying in the same current' was thoroughly compelling. Also summoning Japan to mind, was Maria Isakova Bennet's poem 'With its loud shrill notes, yellow attracted me for a while' because the Japanese expression *kiiroi koe* (黄色 声) or 'yellow voice' denotes the high-pitched voices of women and children.

---

[1] John Paul Caponigro, *60 Great Quotes On Color*, https://www.johnpaulcaponigro.com/blog/16588/60-great-quotes-on-color/

[2] Ted Hughes, *Birthday Letters*, Faber & Faber, 1999

Other poems that really stood out for me were tender depictions of relationships between parent and child, such as Lara Frankena's clever quintet, 'Kindled'. The theme of seeing through a child's eyes also emerged in many poems, such as Nia Broomhall's 'Sky' with 'my tick birds high' and 'stick people smiles in the big wide why' and the charming ekphrastic poem, 'Breughels' by Stephen Payne, where Pieter the Toddler tries to determine exactly what is going on in the painting.

Aside from wonderful poems in a variety of forms, in this issue you will also find Mary Mulholland's interview with Mark Waldron, Julie Irigaray's essay on 'the forgotten bee poems' of Sylvia Plath, and reviews of new titles from Sue Wallace-Shaddad, Julian Bishop, SK Grout, Lesley Sharpe, Tamsin Hopkins and Diana Cant. Our featured poet is Maria Isakova Bennet whose astonishing, concise poems are real gems. You can find the link to her talk on page 53.

It has been my absolute pleasure to guest edit this issue. Thank you so much to everyone who trusted us with their poems and wishing you all the very best with your writing.

Alexandra Corrin-Tachibana

Figure 1 Quince (Cydonia oblonga): fruit, flowers and sectioned fruit. Coloured zincograph, c. 1853, after M. Burnett. Source: Wellcome Collection.

Quince Tree

If you want to see it, the whole universe is contained in a tree
Antonio López García

Antonio López García sketches the quince tree in his courtyard,
each day of September. He marks the fruits with white stripes.
As the branch droops a little lower each day, another line—
and another. He captures the passing of time. The shadows
have light in them; muted yellows and greens. Sometimes,
he sits by a stuccoed wall in the shade. The space is deep
and round. The fruits become heavy with rot and fall. A web
of strings surrounds the tree. He places nails in the ground
to mark the position of his feet where he stands. There is a metal
frame covered in tarpaulin, the centre fixed with a hanging
weight. His two daughters complain. *Poor tree*, they say.
He sketches the spaces around, bright as shards of glass. His marks
show the way the quince darkens, how its skin has split and lost its
bloom. Sometimes, the tight branches cast shadows like the grilles
of a prison. His palette captures the sun through the leaves, clear
and sombre. It is not the dusk's fading light, nor the milky light
of dawn, nor that of a bright afternoon. It is light in action, casting
shadows—like children making shapes on a wall. His two daughters
help the housekeeper pick the yellow fruit. To make membrillo
jelly. She sees the rows of guide lines on the skins.
It's Papa, he marks everything.

Kris Spencer

Inspired by *Dream of Light / El sol del membrillo* (1992), directed by Victor Erice

Silver Birches

On leaving the flat, I always turn left to walk up towards the silver birches. Never right. Because when workmen redid the road, they didn't put back the silver birches here. Well, they put some along the pavement at the posh end of the street, and it's a long street that runs all the way through two neighbourhoods but I mean, come on, the street's called Silver Birch Street! I'm at the not-so-posh end and I don't know why they didn't replace them here as they did there. Maybe the council ran out of money, or the other end of the street fought a better campaign to not cut down the silver birches in the first place, so that those in planning were made fully aware of certain of the residents' emotional attachment to the silver birches. Or maybe it's because the posher part was so vociferous in its opposition to the notification of plans to improve the urban environment (which meant ripping up and relaying the road and pavement) that it put posters up in the windows of the houses on the street that said 'Save our Silver Birches' (even though they were all gnarly and their roots had pushed up the slabs) thus explaining the appearance of newly planted and suitably supported young silver birches up their end. They must surely have lobbied more convincingly to get some sort of reassurance before the work began that saplings of silver birches would one day be replanted. Else those deciding on silver birches, the ones who hold the purse strings for purchasing silver birches, simply thought that posh people have a generally greater appreciation of trees than the rest of us, who can live perfectly well without occasionally spaced silver birches, that we can't possibly have the aesthetic sensibility to appreciate the silvery texture of their trunks and branches, that we prefer empty pavements and more spaces for parking. Maybe they argued that only posh people would know about the silver birch being Finland's national tree and that Finns like to use bunches of birch boughs to beat themselves while bathing in the sauna. Maybe they ascertained that posh people know this because they have the means to go to Finland and would have read it in the guidebook on the plane and booked an excursion to a Finnish forest and when they got back exhausted had a sauna making sure to beat themselves while bathing with their bunch of boughs from silver birches. Yes, maybe the posh people up that end get cleaner than us and are more deserving on hygiene grounds or have less dead skin, are more deserving on exfoliation grounds. It could be simpler than that, and they just have an innate appreciation of silver birches and birches period, like they just happened to be born with a silver birch in their mouth.

Paul Stephenson

September

The coast path near Otterton

By the kissing gate we kiss –
pause to gather blackberries from hedgerows

tangled between summer and autumn.
We stand with our backs to the path

our hands moving up, across, like painters
gauging the sharp perspective of bramble, thorn,

choosing carefully with forefinger, smudged thumb,
each drupel-jewel, black diamond.

The cliff's quiet, the blue sea even.
A breeze plays everywhere

affectionately – my face, your hair.
We don't talk much. Our signing hands

speak for us, anticipating red wine in winter,
berries frozen with the garden's apples.

When I unfold the map
my fingers print our way with purple inks.

Jeff Skinner

The Melancholy Thistle

The Melancholy Thistle appears
in upland meadows in the north,
a solitary flower.

Mauve, the colour of a bruise,
a fingerprint left on a woman's wrist
held too hard.

Spineless, the flower turned potion,
took away sadness for a while,
left a purple haze.

In the mirror her eye violets,
blooms around a red centre,
keeps her indoors.

Jo Colley

Baltic Flour Mill

It wasn't the Baltic Flour Mill.
Nor the Tyne nor its bridges
and their russet spill into the channel.

Your eyes had sipped the Alnmouth sea,
green and pebbled smooth.
I was looking at their light,
and the spun waters of your jumper.

Anthony Tomkins

Figure 2 Driftwood, by Louise Claire Lovell

Broad Haven

Gwen John

Grey; stints of further grey –
brook, meadow, greyed by sea winds
and the sea beyond. But in the grasses are
pinks, primroses, buttery orchids, such claims
on you that on winter days you will spend
what it takes for nosegays, hothouse yellows
like king cups, sun bright.

When Whistler shows you –
how to model grey on grey, to form
the figure as if in clay, with underpainting
gazed upon before the top coats, it will fuse
to this: broad haven. The air itself, the drawn
curtains of fine rains, then flower-starred hedges,
the day's transparent glazes. Sprint lights.

Kathryn Pallant

2019 PANTONE 16-1546 Living Coral An animating and life-affirming coral hue with a golden undertone that energises and enlightens with a softer edge.

Data from nearby drilling projects suggest the Great Barrier Reef is a geological infant. The Cathédrale Notre-Dame de Paris is distinguished by its size, antiquity and architectural interest. Once upon a time, there was a city so dazzling and kaleidoscopic, so braided and water-rimmed, that it was compared to a single living body. Pointed arches and flying buttresses allowed the walls to be soaring and thin. It clustered around a glimmering emerald spine, opened into radiant, iris-coloured avenues, which tourists crossed oceans to see. In the tall light, people felt the presence of God. Then, all at once, a kind of invisible wildfire overran the city. The fire raging through the oak timbers got so hot — almost certainly more than 760 degrees Celsius — that it ate into the adjacent limestone walls and into the tops of some vaults. It consumed its avenues and neighbourhoods, swallowed its canyons and branches. 3D printed interlocking units with a porcelain coating may attract baby coral polyps. *If we rework it the way it was worked, in the same manner and with the same materials, the message can be transmitted,* François Calame, ethnologist, says. *You'll be able to feel it.*

2020 PANTONE® 16-1546 Classic Blue An expansive presence, Classic Blue is evocative of the vast and infinite evening sky opening a world of possibilities.

January 23: Doomsday clock moves to 100 seconds to midnight. Scientists cite two simultaneous existential dangers — nuclear war and climate change — compounded by a threat multiplier, cyber-enabled information warfare, undercutting humanity's capacity to respond. December 31: global deaths from novel-Coronavirus 1,976,810, rising.

Julie Runacres

References

Meyer, Robinson. 'Since 2016, Half of All Coral in the Great Barrier Reef Has Died.' *The Atlantic*, 18 Apr. 2018, www.theatlantic.com/science/archive/2018/04/since-2016-half-the- coral-in-the-great-barrier-reef-has-perished/558302/#. Accessed 11 May 2023.
@NatGeoUK. 'Notre Dame Rises Again.' *National Geographic*, 17 Feb. 2022, www.nationalgeographic.co.uk/history-and civilisation/2022/02/notre-dame-rises-again.
Meehan Crist. 'The Quest to Save Coral Reefs.' *The Atlantic*, 17 Mar. 2016, www.theatlantic.com/science/archive/2016/03/saving-coral-reefs/473844
Bulletin of the Atomic Scientists. (n.d.).2020 statement [online] Available at: https://thebulletin.org/doomsday-clock/2020-doomsday-clock-statement/.
https://www.worldometers.info/coronavirus/coronavirus-death-toll/
WorldOMeter. 'Coronavirus Death Toll Update - *Worldometer*.' Worldometers.info, Worldometer, 2022, www.worldometers.info/coronavirus/coronavirus-death-toll

Winchcombe, August 2020

That afternoon the sunshine
baked all the colour from the scene.
                                                            The Hercules

appeared, a hundred feet above
the street – the four propellor engines
placed it fifty years ago, on a painted plate
in a children's picture book.
                                                            Cars had vanished,

the road was empty, the road was wider.
The pubs were closed. The little town
stunned by the heat from another country,
the surprise of the plane.

Benedict Newbery

Bougainvillea

When I think of that year
it's bougainvillea that comes back,
so called because the Frenchman
found it on his travels, because
it is tropical, outrageous,
belonging to another world
more flamboyant, joy-filled,
extravagant than ours, but also
because I can still see it spilling
those red, papery flowers
over the porch of that villa
in Portugal where days were spent
sunbathing in a garden, dropping
into a pool when the heat was too much.
I was swimming towards you
at the deep end that summer and surely
the flowers could not be real?
Only a child could imagine that colour.

Carole Bromley

Figure 3 Artist's Pigments, Venice, by Roger Camp

Breughels

The Peasant Dance, 1568

Pieter the toddler is standing next to Pieter the father, who is finishing a painting. Big Pieter names the colours on his palette and talks about the people who are wearing them. There are so many colours in this painting, and so much for a child to look at, with the characters so full of beans, a drama in every part of the panel. Little Pieter loves the big red flag, and he loves the dancing, the party of limbs. The yellow of the peasant woman's apron. The red and yellow halves of the Jester's costume. He wonders if the couple at the doorway are saying hello or goodbye. Then he spots the grey and white bird on a windowsill. Does it want to enter the building? If he'd done the painting, he would know.

Stephen Payne

Alice Blue Gown

for her wedding
she chose blue
like the songs
we sang to you
exquisite daughter
proud inside
under the scrutiny
of *every eye*
rare as sodalite
moon's third eye
volcano's fire
and siren's sigh
malurus splendens
watch them fly
nosegay bouquet
of Jackman's rue
borrowed necklace
from one who knew
sapphire for wisdom
to herald the new
gentle gentian
passion ensues
tiny trumpet
little boy blew
thistle, ocean,
dart frog, sky
mourning to glory
bye and bye

Cheryl Moskowitz

Sky

My every sky then was a brushblue line
across the top of the paper. My skies
were far and up away from empty white
where things lived, my round clouds, my tick birds high
over pointy roofs of houses like mine,
green lines for grass and yellow sun that shined
and stick people smiles in the big wide why
of world I had no colours for but white.
One afternoon before my picture dried
Mrs Gadd said *look out there, see, the sky*
goes all the way down and I looked outside
at the willow field and my wide-eyed find
that blue through branches was still the sky. My
brush washed my paper with green and blue light.

Nia Broomhall

Studio, morning

(after Roger Robinson)

and if I speak of painting
I speak of stepping in

break into the reds
corner the greens
yield to the yellows
mix ochre with grey

I speak of the touch of tube
oily sweat of pigment
cold silver

feather of brush
flex, dab, spring

I speak of the easel
slotted, propped
balanced
slipped
gripped to order

stains flavour the air
faint resin of paint
crunch of charcoal
feel of white coat
its poppered wrists

I hum a hymn
from childhood, graze the dry
canvas with the palm of my hand

the sound of the door behind me
forgotten
swinging loose

Deb Catesby

In Ordinary Time

with that green altar cloth after Trinity
an angle where the sun
soaks through a south window
dissolving six detailed saints
and polite martyrdoms

to a smudge of haloes
blurred across tired stones –
illegible, foot-flattened,
their coats of arms and names
smoothed out of history –
to become
the surviving spirits of colour,
free and abstract and liquid
glowing with life.

D A Prince

The Colours of Jesus

Jesus can walk on anything;
on stones, over grit and brown earth,
he can glide on the heavenly welcome of skies,
skim lightly over blue waters
in new Birkenstocks
and garments the colour of butter;

he slipped into my nightmare last night
without asking,
rattled over brittle ridges of baked sand
in his old Ford Cortina,
bounced dust off clay covered pipelines,
past flares of orange from towers of oil,
like he was speeding through scenes
from a movie about black gold.

He paused when he saw me.
I think he wanted to lend a helping hand
as I bent under the redness of a half dark sky,
the shade you might see on a fading rose
before it gives up.
I was hanging my head,
cradling a plastic bag
given to me by a bearded stranger.
It dripped scarlet
that congealed to a flaky black
on the surface of desert sands.

The robes of Jesus glowed yellow
like a cactus flower after rain.
He motioned to me
to get on over there, like we were old friends
catching up to stroll into the flood
that lay between us like a mirage.

And I walked out into that ocean
and gave it all up –
the sticky bag, the black dog, my white lies.

Patrick Agnew

Pentimenti

Marks of repentance
float to the surface
through layered oils,
ochre and ultramarine
thinning, dulled.

An original outline
returns as a second
coming, emerging
like the faith
which doubt erased

or the shape of a love
whitewashed out
in a deliberate act
of forgetting.
A gesture transpires.

Stained by what's gone,
the present moment
blears your bright denials.

Fiona Larkin

Green

Lime olive pea grass
green from my heart's core
kesk grün glas vert
come back. Bring us rain
callow sweet supple tender
ntsuab yaşil akhdar kanach
come back when the clouds
downy raw spick breezy
carry water back home.

Sleep on the ground floor,
pale ashy waxen wan
dampen all your stale clothes,
drought parch thirst burn
drink, store what you can
simple minded credulous
make us wet behind the ears
unpolished, gullible,
let us be born yesterday.

In an overheating world
swaddled by an atmosphere
warm as amniotic fluid
let me cool you in a dress
blue as summer, soaking wet.
Put the dress on, round world,
feel the hairs on your skin
rise with coolness, singing.
World, free yourself of us.

Sarah Mnatzaganian

Trace

The stencil spells the word MISSING.
She unwraps it every morning
from white tissue, holds it up

to the light, considers frosting
the lettering to a glazed door,
in private eye movie-style.

She thinks about dabbing the word
to a road sign, ice-sifting it
over Victoria sponge.

She wonders about chalk-dusting
leisure centre walls, Tippexing
over posters in the mall.

One day, she pours her tea through, space
by space, then the milk for the cat,
water for the garden birds.

She finds a tiny sample pot
of Borrowed Light, the palest paint.
Finds it too much. At the window

she takes a deep breath, and stencils
the air, feels the breeze trace her
—

Oenone Thomas

White Room

Greenland, 1960

The procedure room is bright.
Her body is surveyed
by something

coated white and gloved
reflecting in the lamps above.
She is pinioned

on repeat, stirruped in steel.
Trying to stay silent
and so still.

She counts skips.
The rope swings overhead,
white against mute sky,

each girl takes her turn,
slipping through the white space
of the lie.

They sing their cool clear notes,
instruments of ice,
an aqaat flaring

in Ilulisatt's sterile light.
Salt stings the skin,
every time they jump

and land.
Her small hand holds
the white sheet, under which

she quietly burns,
knuckle-white, breath-white.
Later, nobody takes turns

to ask why,
she is sitting in the snow
trying not to cry

Lauren Thomas

A Dress So Beautiful it Would Wear You to Death

The moment she steps from the carriage she knows the world sees her. Her exquisite emerald tarlatan outshines the dead-stone jewels the others wear. In the ballroom she will burn, gas-light bright, scorching her rivals' pale silks and sombre bombazines.

In the attics and the piece-work rooms, the girls dust down the dresses. White arsenic and copper make the brightest hue. The powder coats their arms, drifts down to the holes in their shoes; in the places it lands, the ulcers form. Scabs and sores ignored as long as the fabric is delivered. They vomit in viridian shades, though the blood they bring up is still scarlet.

Breathless from more than the tightness of her corset, she spends her last night dancing. So thrilled by the envious faces that surround her, she does not know that her own eyes gleam with the deadliest shade of fashionable green.

Penny Blackburn

The Killing Jars

That long summer all the boys in our street became
lepidopterists. Armed with fishing nets we caught
them in fields, gardens, parks and the cliffs around town –
Red Admirals, Orange Tips, Brimstones, Green-veined Whites,
Common Blues, Purple Hairstreaks – all enjoying
their fleeting moment in the sun. We took them home,
anxious not to damage our delicate gold.

There we put them into the killing jars that Beak,
our biology master, had shown us how to make:
freshly crushed laurel leaves releasing hydrogen
cyanide in the bottom of screw-top jam jars.
In three days they were dead and we mounted
our specimens on display boards, pinned and labelled
like more exotic species in the town museum.

But in time the potency of laurel leaf poison falls
until they merely stun. Then the day came when
one of our pinioned butterflies began to flap;
and that was that. The football season started
so we went back to collecting players' autographs.

Dave Martin

The Pinks I Have Not Lived

As a bridesmaid, sweating and constricted
I have not felt pretty in synthetic blush.

My workdays have not warranted the promise
of a power suit in cerise.

During my wildest nights, I have not lived
the neon pink adventurousness of a Tracey Emin sign.

Even in heels, my hooves have not mastered
the salmon pink arch of a Barbie's foot.

Though I have not lived these pinks, I have known
the pink-red early signs of unwanted periods,
heat in my cheeks – the pink of the unrequited –
and the 5am pink hue few wake to see in the sky.

Frances Rose O'Leary

Figure 4 Lighting up the moon, by Sultana Raza

The Shrine of Santa Christina

Pebbles in the blue lagoon tell the history of sardines. The scent of brine rolls onto the rocks and up the hillside. Wicker sandals on caramel feet, dry lips, hungry fingers genuflecting under the sun.

She died for your sins.

The holy water is warm as a midwinter bath but still crowds of sunburnt foreheads plummet beneath its surface, dancing moonstones on the mudbrick roof. Redemption burns red on the mountain, stained glass reflects blooming pastures onto the pews. The swell of clouds over the ocean tell them the catch will be rich.

Alice Eaves

Had I The Wings

Swallows swell in the throat of a Traveller girl.
Her eyes closed to the rolling fields
with their caravan green lit by the dash of clouds.
The small squares of a ghost train where a man
in a fedora paints the stage enclosed
by the rattling roof of small wheels turning.

She sings of black sheep, the grief of a woman
cast out upon the roads, her child stolen.
The old gypsy curse to become a swan
lost at sea. Homesickness humming
in her bones. How for a few pennies
in a seashell, she will take you
a thousand miles across the ocean.

The carriage on fire with the fiddler's lament.
How this is the year he discovered colour
as the new frontier. Light itself a bow
across the strings. Feathers in air.
The crackle of the seat's plumage.
How she does not sing for him
or anyone but leaps between the stops.

Music on the wing. How to catch that
low evening sun in the collar of her coat.
The last train out of Dublin. A theatre
of orange where all is fleeting glimpses,
invisible passengers. A freedom far beyond
this island of dirty laundry with its silent prisons,
where the sorrow of skin on skin is buried passion
in a black bag slung on to the rack of sin.

No wonder they went mad. Only the lyrics
hold the mirage of being welcomed back
into a small town when she has been branded
beggar, whore, filthy tinker. Only the painter
hears her dignity, how she rides the railroad,
ticketless as a nightingale. A tune so old
it's wild with the burning hues of dusk,
the swirl of his brush, her journey's end.

Aoife Mannix

Blue Sail

Why does she name only one thing –
the sail on the boat, names only what
without naming we would be least

aware of? Not red of shoe, green
of stem, cornflower jug, plum of anemone,
lemon of lemon, not pink, vivid,

almost fuchsia bench and backdrop
of plaster, not floor, hint of mauve,
nor depth of keel.

Maria Isakova Bennett

With its loud shrill notes, yellow attracted me for a while

Later, I heard that yellow is the colour
of madness. And it's true.

It was a desperate year. Now it's green –
which of course is blue at heart

but needs yellow – something jasmine
or wing of goldfinch.

As penance,
I slather Berlin blue on my walls.

Maria Isakova Bennett

Cafe Caravaggio

1592 – 1600 ***Cappuccino***
Great drink to get going.
Colour of a Capuchin friar's cloak.
Thick foam floats over a darker layer beneath.
Often served with a precarious heart etched on froth.

1600 – 1606 ***Macchiato Longo***
Italian for long stain, a reference to the mark left
by steamed milk when dashed into the coffee.
Distinct layers of cream and buff.
Rich texture, robust and bold.

1606 – 1610 ***Espresso (doppio)***
Best direct from the Gaggia.
Seething water forced through a dark roast of grounds.
Potent brew, immediate rush to the head.
Grits cling to the cup.

Julian Bishop

Resurrection

had I known her
we would have considered
the luminosity of blue

crushed lapis, inks of violets
and indigo, the shifting hues of woad,
feathers snipped from wings of jays,
aizome

but she was already gone

appalled at the simplicity of it
the absurdly quiet ending

I am shocked by the taste of salt
by my weight in the water

my saltburn eyes see nothing
but the waves' black light

I grow weary of the cold
the tilt and slam of ocean

I draw maps with bitten fingers
float them,

will myself towards the coast,
its roar of shingle

I grow weary of the cold

I watch her uncurling:
a stunned bird

the tumbling in slow motion
through layers of darkness
and microscopic life

planets escaping from her mouth
hold words I do not understand

I send angels to rescue her
from the deep and restless tide

had I known you
we could have considered
the greatness of the sea
held back by the high windows

filling the church
with its underwater light

filling the church
while we sit and pray
and breathe

and breathe

the blue air

Jane Lovell

colourfast

my mother is the colour of builder's tea / of wet
grass that hasn't yet had time to thirst for more rain / my mother
is the colour of lucky coal brought in by a stranger on new
year's eve / she carries three droplets of ocean / the colour
of an early June evening under the skin on her wrist

my father is the colour of strong coffee / a shot
bitter / drunk at the bar as it should be / my father
is the colour of marble church floors echoing with footsteps
of believers heading for the altar / he is monochrome
lights on a tree felled from a real forest / roots cut loose

my brother was electric / purple and bright thumping
in his chest / mad green under his fingernails / my brother
was blue as a hot summer's day / the one we ran through before
we had bodies / before they were stained / my brother
was buried in a red blazer / neither his favourite colour nor his favourite coat

Dillon Jaxx

Camera Obscura

In the living room crackly radio static transfigures
into 'I'll be Seeing You' just as winter bursts indoors
and wrecks all domesticity. From the hallway
the sound of low cries – incantations, soft pleas
enough to curse a house. Mother tells me they send
little boys to deliver the telegrams like ants
carrying thousands of times their own weight.
Years later, sitting in a darkened room with a lens
and mirror embedded in the roof, I act as God's spy
to consider the scene on the table, a fast-flowing
river of people. For a moment, I think I see
my smiling brother slip into a Cadillac, only
for his image to burn out like acetate melting
on a film reel, disappear into bright white tundra.
But by then, I know grief is a type of ensnarement
all attempts to escape just tighten the wire.

Fiona Perry

Salary Man

A Japanese job is won in a blue-clad interview,
carried out in black, white and conformity
till even dreams lose their hue.

Long hours in the office. On the train home
their bodies are sea anemones swaying in the same current.
I want them to sit, the black trouser legs to lift

like the lid coming off a sealed tin,
a glimpse of colourful socks
dandelions breaking through tarmac.

L B Jørgensen

your old brown brogues

your old brown brogues
defy time — I twist open
a tin of Cherry Blossom
paste the grease thick

on old brown bristles
leather against my hand
I push loose circles
you appraise with a nod

soft as a hand fluttering
at paper, then the buff
fast and light —
similar to your feet

sliding across parquet
floors — old brown soles
would have slipped, worn
thin from jiving

at the dances thirteen
pints of black stout
wait to be blessed —
a clergy beside

and the showbands
quickening hearts
all toe-tap grins —
sweat and tobacco

old brown shoes
polished to sunset
fading to brown night
they'll do alright

for the dancing

Ian Irwin

Things that quicken the heart

Email from the lab with my blood tests.
Immune Thrombocytopenia torpedoing
my teeming, red forest. Words not making
anything stop, how the day carries on.
The body mistaking a seedling for war.
An unknown path opening up in the bed.
How it comes to a premature end.
Garnet beads strewn towards another way home.

Vasiliki Albedo

Struck home

Tonight we bury everything I've ever said where
the elm tree bends its trunk. Sometimes you make me
drink mud – throat sodden, heavy as a grave.
You tell me it's best I'm quiet, how it suits me, your

hand on my neck where it smarts. You're sure
my silence makes you love me more and I'm to visit
my grave, barefoot, because who needs shoes when
it's not that cold, when even the snow silently melts?

You tell me about my ice-hard heart and how you
held it in the kindling cup of your palms, softened me
so I whimpered like a weaning pup. And you smile, your
thumb and finger pinching my cheek, how pale I am,

you say, no wonder nobody looks… no wonder nobody…
no wonder. It's not the unfairness of it that cakes
my tongue, but how my words suspend themselves
like the black head of a shackled horse.

Abegail Morley

Kindled

My daughter's near-black hair is lit
with undertones of fire.
When I tuck a strand behind her ear
she shrugs me off,
rakes her fingers through embers.

Lara Frankena

Peploe in Cassis

Hôtel Panorama. And to think
I was reluctant to bring William here
with his pale colouring and pigmentation.
It's everything a wintry Scotland isn't
with sun and sunlight, warmth and colour.
We celebrated young Bill's third birthday
not with Champagne but with Lafite.
Château Lafite. Why not?
The Mediterranean colours are so bright
the light is dazzling seen through spectacles,
the sunshine glinting scintillating sun.

I smell the rosemary in the *maquis*
and feel the crisp floor of brown pine needles
in their V-shapes springy on the sand-hot ground.
Limestone *calanques* glow and in the harbour
multi-coloured flotillas of fishing boats
are painting their own reflections
on wavelets sidling in the harbour water.
The Roman orange terracotta tiles
shine on roofs bright against cerulean skies.
What colour are those shadows? Purple? Blue?

And everywhere we hear French words
in accents Provençal and Occitan,
the salty speech of fishermen mending nets
and smells of bread baked daily:
ficelle, baguette, brioche.
The market sells fresh fruits:
oranges, lemons, grapes and green-striped melons
with many oval seeds to be scooped out
of orange-bearded and sun-sweetened flesh.
A bottle of local white wine lies wedged in a rockpool
to cool among the sea anemones and shrimps.
And all day long cicadas rasp and sing.
I paint and paint until the sun goes down,
that glowing orb of fire unquenched by sea
where moonlight takes its nightly moonlit swim.

Duncan Forbes

Orange nasturtiums against a dark wall

bring to mind Moroccan chocolate,
black coffee, the possibilities of thick cream.
The room is curtained alcoves,

voices are mutter, music is bouzoukia,
chairs are cushions, flowers lean
over a curvaceous vase, strain to listen

as we do to each other. We need our hands
to talk. Darkness surrounds us.
We draw closer, let lips read lips.

Maria Isakova Bennett

The Colours of Still Life

(after N Scott Momaday's *The Colors of Night)*

1. White

It's twelve tender asparagus tips grown starved of light and tied with twine. It's nothingness, void, emptiness, bleak eternity but without it there'd be no light reflecting on the wine goblets, no shimmer in the hairs of hung rabbits, no glistening olives, no oysters. It is every star in the sky, twinkle in an eye, every perfect snowflake. It was the moonlight streaming in through the window, your hand on my thigh telling me I was beautiful.

2. Red

It's the lobster on a silver charger, four crisp apples and a knife, a pomegranate cut in two. It is danger, a warning, a bar brawl, a thief's hands. It is the monster hiding under the bed in 50s America. It provokes bulls and terrifies footballers. It is a knife down a dark alley. It is the devil, lust, sex, power. It is hot. It is a fast car. It is a heart-shaped chocolate box, a lucky bridal gown, a kiss on an envelope, a lollipop. It is remembrance. It is a heavy ache inside for you.

3. Yellow

It's a lemon peeled and sliced on a plate. It's three joyful round bellied pears. It's gold's understudy. Mustard gas, pus, jaundice, Mount Vesuvius' sulphur clouds. It is cowardice. It is a slur. It was the book under Oscar Wilde's arm. It is the colour in a flag. It is pride. It is hope. It is bath stone, warm syrup on porridge, positivity. It is a carousel at the carnival, childhood summers remembered, and the most fun I'd ever had with you in Bloemendaal.

4. Purple

It's five pert little figs, a punnet of plums, a goblet of wine lit up by candlelight. It is opulence, forbidden, Jenny Joseph's *Warning*. It is the sky before a storm, wisdom, a blood clot in a gusset, the crown chakra. It is a dance round my bedroom, a brave heart, berry stains on a white skirt. It is Autumn's bounty, the colour I remember my grandmother by. A fresh bruise on my eye to keep me inside, because I was *too beautiful.*

5. Brown

It's the hard, furrowed brains of walnuts in a pewter bowl. It's the earthenware jug of ale, the brace of pheasants. It is filth, shit, silt and soil. It is the sludge that we get when all colours are mixed. It is where we end. It saves the hunted from predators. It is a warm cardigan, Italian leather brogues, the best Oxford libraries. It is contentment. It is home for the tortoise. It is me and my babies snuggled in the same bed.

6. Black

It's the dead eyes of a bird on the table, mussels in their shells, a dish of grapes like polished opals. It's the start of life and the end. It is blankness. It's an expression of light, but not light. It's everything wicked: witches, the occult, Anish Kapoor's controversy. It is Chanel's LBD, it's cool, it's prestige. It is a cloak I wore for too many years. It is our scapegoat, but it unassumingly enhances every still life and without it stars wouldn't shine as bright.

Elle Stear

The Reading

Watch the Video

Maria Isakova Bennett reads and discusses her poems 'Blue Sail', 'With its loud shrill notes, yellow attracted me for a while' and 'Orange nasturtiums against a dark wall' which you will find on pages 37, 38 and 50

The Alchemy Spoon
YouTube Channel

https://youtu.be/y-yTmfkx1f8

The Interview

Poet and tutor **Mark Waldron** started writing poetry in his forties while working in advertising and has since published five collections. **Mary Mulholland** talks to Mark about his writing practice.

MM: I find something unsettling in your poetry, so perhaps we can start with something safe, like your origins: you were born in New York – did that have an influence?

MW: No. I left when I was about six weeks old. But maybe when you know you come from somewhere else, it does affect the way you see yourself. When I was young, I recall feeling it gave me two perspectives.

MM: But you don't consider yourself American?

MW: Well, I have two passports, but that culture didn't have time to get inside me. I remember going back to New York in my twenties, thinking: am I going to feel some distant vestigial connection? I fantasised that I did, but it was probably only in my mind.

MM: At that stage were you already keen on American poetry? I've seen Ashbery and Berryman are flagged up as being important to you.

MW: They are important to me, but not really as influences, because I was already doing what I was doing before I knew their work. It's a bit embarrassing to compare yourself with people of that stature, but when I discovered them, I thought 'oh, they're somewhere way up ahead on the road I might have wanted to go down'. But the poets I was exposed to as a child were mostly from the UK.

MM: You've said somewhere the writers you discovered in your teens, like TS Eliot and Virginia Woolf, are the ones who stay with you. How would you say they influenced you?

MW: My mother got me to read *The Waves* in my teens, and I thought: Wow, you can do this with language! I found that incredibly exciting. And TS Eliot, well, the way he'd switch registers, or a nursery rhyme would come out of nowhere, and employing different voices: he seemed to be having fun. I didn't go to university, so I'm looking back to what I was exposed to doing my A levels, and what my parents introduced me to.

MM: Were your parents literary, did they encourage you?

MW: They both loved literature. My mother had aspirations to be a writer. She was published in *Punch*, and tried many times for *The New Yorker* and had other articles published in fashion magazines. She loved Virginia Woolf and Katherine Mansfield. My parents would take us to Beckett plays at the Royal Court in the 70s when we were teenagers.

MM: So, did you go straight from A levels to advertising?

MW: I went from A levels to dropping out. I did lots of different jobs, before knuckling down with a proper job. Not that advertising is a proper job I suppose...

MM: What do you enjoy about advertising – you're a copywriter, right?

MW: Coming up with ideas, it's a nice feeling.

MM: And wordplay?

MW: Ideas really. Maybe in poetry too, it's the ideas that are appealing.

MM: It'd be interesting to hear where your ideas come from, and if it's a parallel thing for poetry: do you start with a prompt, go for a walk...?

MW: In advertising, if you don't come up with enough ideas that are successful you're out of a job. And you work in a team with an art director. So eventually I'd say to my partner, *I give up, I can't crack this brief.* Then I'd walk out of the room and I'd be standing at the urinal say, and suddenly it'd come, and I'd think *god, that's it!* – as if in the moment of letting go and giving up, ideas come. Wrestling with something is not conducive to ideas. Or maybe you have to wrestle first, but the idea won't emerge till later. I don't know if that's a parallel with poetry – unless you've been commissioned and will have to perform (and you don't want to make a fool of yourself), poetry's a lot less pressure.

MM: What does poetry give you that copywriting doesn't?

MW: Certainly not money. Maybe it has more respect in the world. After estate agents, politicians, and maybe arms dealers, advertising is one of the most despised professions. So I guess poetry might give some people a sense of self-worth. There's a little pocket of society that admires people who do poetry for some reason. It's a tiny pocket, but there's nobody who admires people who do ads.

MM: I was wondering how you ended up with a poem like 'Blossom'. Did it come out like that? How much workshopping do you do?

MW: I did workshops for sixteen years – with Michael Donaghy for a few years, then John Stammers, Roddy Lumsden, but I've done almost none for about seven years...

MM: You'll probably say it varies, but how many drafts might you do?

MW: In my new book, with the fairy tale poems, once I had that idea, the rest was easy. Once you have an idea for a theme you're like a miner who's found a seam of coal. But there are others where it's taken me maybe a hundred drafts, and then I've given it up, or gone back to it six months later, or find I've got half a poem, then realise something else I did five years ago is also half a poem, and maybe I could steal from that one and stick them together...

MM: Can you give an example of one that came easily and one you laboured over?

MW: 'The life cycle of the fly,' from the *Itchy Sea* is one I laboured over. I had lots of poems about flies, with bits I knew were good, but lots of bits I felt weren't good enough, so I chopped them all up and cobbled it together. Another from that collection came from a prompt and was pretty easy: I had in mind a car made of chocolate, then thought it wasn't going to work as there was air inside this chocolate car. Then I thought, the empty spaces could be made of chocolate too! That was when I realised I had a poem, and it was really simple to write, as everything could be made out of this substance. But 'The life cycle of the fly' has a bunch of different ideas, so that inevitably takes longer...

MM: Would you say the advertising world has influenced you in creating your videos, for example, reciting poems in a Wendy house?[3]

---

[3] https://www.bloodaxebooks.com/ecs/product/a-straight-up-giant-1326

MW: I don't think so. I did those films of myself reciting because I memorise everything, and I thought: if they're already in my head and I don't have to learn them, I might as well stick the camera on.

There are things from advertising about communication that I carry into poetry. I might have an idea for an ad and tell my creative director and he'll say 'I've absolutely no idea what you're talking about'. That's why workshops are useful: what makes total sense in your own head doesn't necessarily communicate beyond that realm.

MM: You seem to be able to step into your unconscious, a bit like how a child does, though your imagination often has a darkness, as if there's an existential angst beneath the absurd, as in for example 'death is not what you think it is, it's what I think it is'[4]. Can you say something about this?

MW: I remember my mother saying, 'I quite like your poetry but too much of it is about death'. I suppose I'm interested in where darkness and funniness meet, the poignancy where these things touch each other. And I am certainly interested in pushing boundaries about what is acceptable, as, for example, in 'The Dead are Helpless'[5] where dead bodies are being treated badly. I remember an interview where Charles Simic asked James Tate how he worked, and Tate said he steps into this surreal world, trusting something true would emerge. That's something I try to do too, I think. You set off and hope for the best.

I don't know what the darkness is about, except don't we all have dark places that are unresolved, and we pick at those scabs?... Also we're going to die.

MM: And that's what makes your poems more than surreal and funny. We need the shadows or everything looks flat.

Another thing about your poems is your use of the persona, which I guess is like a way of looking at the multifaceted parts of ourselves – as you say, 'All poems are an advertisement for me'. In 'Burn Down', you look at yourself through ironic asides.

MW: Roddy Lumsden once said to me 'Why don't you try to write poems about yourself?' and I remember thinking I'm suspicious about there being some kind of solid self that you can write from. It's a construction, just as a persona is a construct. If you dress up as characters, as a woman,

---

[4] 'All My Poems are Advertisements For Me', from *Meanwhile, Trees* (Bloodaxe, 2016)
[5] ibid.

or a fox, or a puppet dog or whatever, you can come upon sides of yourself that are otherwise hidden.

MM: You do this in 'The Woodman Prince', where changes occur and the character shifts with 'an arbitrary frequency'. I'd also love to hear more about your use of sound play, in 'broom, broom' or 'fee, fi, fo, and no fun': did you have fun writing this?

MW: Yes, though I think it annoys some people. It's not just a sprinkling of silliness, it's a feeling of trying to communicate through silliness.

MM: Is this something about not taking life too seriously?

MW: Partly, but also making fun of the way people talk. I think in 'Contingency', with the 'broom broom, cha cha', I'm slightly taking the mickey out of the middle class, 'ok yah!' I'm not sure anyone would pick that up of course. I'm conscious of having a middle class accent myself, and because of that, I found it funny and kind of subversive to do a version of it in a poem.

MM: You're also subversive in your use of adjectives. In classes we're often told to get rid of adjectives and adverbs. I'm thinking of 'gone off', when you write 'an under the table mediaevalist' and revel in language. I'd like to hear more about this.

MW: I do like pulling language about: I like dragging stuff from its context and sticking it with words it doesn't belong with. There's a bit in the mediaevalist poem: 'is that you I saw befrolicking off in the betown besquare' which is purposely misusing the 'be' suffix. That's one kind of nonsense I like. One of the things that appeals to me about poetry, especially in this country, where it's a bit hide-bound by convention, you can have fun: it's just waiting for someone to take the mickey out of it!

MM: I also notice you often use a French word ... slip in an *avec*.

MW: I remember deliberately misusing *avec* in 'the trees are done avec their leaves', because the French don't use *avec* the way we use *with*. There are other European languages I play with, too. I did a poem, 'Las Aves Vacías'. I don't speak Spanish, but I thought even if no one likes the poem, if I gave it a Spanish title, they might at least like that bit of it. It adds a flavour to a poem that would be blander without it. If you're

English you look up to French culture as more sophisticated. So you can make fun of that by misusing a bit of French – or Spanish...

MM: Also, in your latest collection, you have a lot of italicised untitled poems – what's their role?

MW: Books change a lot over the time of writing. When I started, I had in mind *The Waves* and the italicised prose bits Woolf has at the start of each chapter or section; the prose is incredibly poetic, whereas the italicised sections are more straightforward, describing sunrise to sunset. I thought I could borrow this structure. Originally, I was also going to include characters from her book. But whenever I have a grand idea like that, it falls apart at some point, and this is just a remnant of that idea.

Then I realised I quite liked the idea of letting the poems in this book, a lot of which don't make much sense, like 'Contingency', intersperse with prose bits in italics, which would give the poems some more solid grounding, and even if the reader didn't get it, these italicised bits would be partly referring to the process. I started thinking I could write poetry that's very loose, and the reader could use the poems as a kind of net to catch their own meaning. So, on one hand I was writing poems some of which are very unstructured and nonsensey, but in prose bits I was talking, sideways, about what I was doing in these poems.

MM: I notice the form of your poetry seems to have become freer. *The Itchy Sea* had more couplets, tercets, freer. Now it's ...

MW: all over the place! I've never been that interested in form, but I started wanting to abandon punctuation so I replaced some of the work punctuation does with form.

MM: What I get from your poems is a bit like 'Endgame': we stay very much in a place, exploring it in many dimensions. Would you say that's what you're doing?

MW: Whether you intend it or not you always finish up with each book coming from its own place, and I think that probably did happen with this; yes, there's a lot in this book about the process, but it's interesting.

I was talking to Joe Dunthorne and he said one of the themes of these poems is change, he mentioned 'The Woodman Prince', his flicking back and forth. I said I hadn't noticed. These are things you notice later.

MM: That's also what you do with your Marcie and Dougal personas, and others slipping into other parts...

MW: Yes. I think most poets only have one or two subjects that they come at from many different angles. They are always worrying at the same bone. It's probably true for me.

MM: What you're really good at is illustrating that nothing is fixed. Maybe that's why I felt unsettled. I note you end the book with 'Nothing', having started with 'Panic Room' – are you a panicky person?

MW: I probably am quite panicky. I remember doing a reading at Cork festival last year, and someone came up afterwards saying 'great reading, but it was terrifying'. I asked what he meant, and he said 'I was terrified what you'd say next'. I never set out to terrify, but if you inhabit different characters you can say whatever you like because none of it's you... I can get panicky that what my characters want to say is unacceptable.

MM: Though somewhere you say...

MW: It's all me! That's the trouble with interviews! I read them afterwards and think I can't believe I said that because I believe the exact opposite.

MM: Somewhere you also said that 'writing is a neurotic activity'!

MW: I mentioned the man in Cork, because the panicky feeling is in the constructing of these things: can I get away with this?

MM: Is that why you include the ironic asides or a 'fee fi fo, no fum' to show you're only playing?

MW: I prefer inhabiting a place of uncertainty where nobody knows what's true, because that better reflects the world I live in...

MM: Going back to an earlier thought, what advice would you give to poets who start later on, for example balancing creative writing with family and work?

MW: If you work as a creative in advertising, at least in in the late 90s, you'd be given a brief and could practically crack it in an hour then you'd still have seven hours to write! It's good to have a job with a computer. I imagine it's getting harder now though. We're living in a horrendous surveillance culture.

I would advise doing workshops. I couldn't have started writing without them. You need to have a sense of what other people are doing, not to copy them, but because you will probably be ignored if you don't tune into what poetry looks like at any given time.

Also, you're in an environment of people doing the same thing. I read a lot of American poets and follow them on Instagram and see what they are doing. I'd advise doing that because it's often more exciting than what's being written here. Having said that, a friend of mine reckons I fetishize American poetry.

MM: What do you think American poets have that we don't?

MW: I heard Mark Ford saying British poetry has always been a continuum, Tennyson to Hardy to Auden to Larkin, whereas American poetry is a series of revolutions, it's more iconoclastic, Whitman, Wallace Stevens, Eliot, Ashbery. I'm drawn to people who want to tear it up and start again. Like Woolf perhaps.

MM: With your poetry, what are your writing plans?

MW: I actually hate the time immediately after a book comes out – because there's always a period, for me at least, of writing stuff that doesn't seem to work. At the moment I have three or four books on the go, each heading uncertainly down a different track. Something will emerge eventually though I'm sure. It always has so far.

Mary Mulholland

<u>Publications by Mark Waldron</u>

The Brand New Dark (Salt, 2008)
The Itchy Sea (Salt, 2011)
Meanwhile, Trees (Bloodaxe, 2016)
Sweet like Rinky-Dink (Bloodaxe, 2019)
A Straight Up Giant (Bloodaxe, 2023)

The Essay

Julie Irigaray explores one of Sylvia Plath's forgotten bee poems, 'The Swarm.'

In the autumn of 1962, Sylvia Plath put together the poetry collection that would become *Ariel.* The version we mostly know today is the one edited by Ted Hughes, who did not keep some poems. However, Plath herself had reservations about one of the poems from her bee poems sequence: 'The Swarm.' On the flyleaf of the manuscript, she put this poem in parentheses, probably to discard it later.[1]

Written on October 7, 1962, 'The Swarm' looks out of place, so it is easy to understand Plath's editorial choice. The extended metaphor of the bees/French troops and the man/Napoleon sustained throughout the poem contrasts too much with Plath's other bee poems, which are more personal. Unlike 'The Bee Meeting', 'The Arrival of the Bee Box', 'Stings' and 'Wintering', which focus on the speaker's experience of beekeeping, Plath does not use the pronoun 'I' in 'The Swarm'. She keeps her distance from the unfolding scene.

The opening scene recalls a battlefield – the speaker can hear someone opening fire in their town. They wonder if it is a crime of passion since 'Jealousy can open the blood', perhaps a reference to Plath's recent discovery of her husband's affair. It is unclear who the fighters are, but the speaker claims: 'It is you the knives are out for / At Waterloo, Waterloo, Napoleon'. In March 1962, Plath was asked to review a biography of Napoleon's wife Josephine for *The New Statesman*, a book she enjoyed reading.[2] This, combined with her interest in European history, probably inspired the parallels between the swarm and the Great Army on one hand, and the man and Napoleon on the other. Indeed, one of the symbols of Napoleon's Empire was the bee because bees gather around one leader (their queen).

The bees rebel against a man who is trying to turn them out. This inexperienced individual, who is visibly neither a professional nor an amateur beekeeper, is ready to get rid of them by any means. The bees must die because the man decided so. In 'The Arrival of the Bee Box', Plath writes: 'They can die, I need feed them nothing, I am the owner' and 'Tomorrow I will be sweet God, I will set them free.' Like Napoleon, the

---

[1] Plath, Sylvia, *Ariel: The Restored Edition* (London: Faber & Faber, 2013).

[2] Plath, Sylvia, *The Letters of Sylvia Plath volume II: 1956-1963*, ed. Peter K. Steinberg and Karen V. Kukil (London: Faber & Faber, 2018). Letter to Aurelia Schober Sylvia Plath, 4th March, p. 734.

man suffers from hubris. Plath judiciously compares the way the man treats the bees to the way Napoleon treated his Great Army ('These are chess people you play with'): it is estimated that between 800,000 and one million Frenchmen died across Europe for his Empire.[3]

The mention of Russia and the expression 'the furnace of greed' is an allusion to Napoleon's thirst for greatness when he invaded this country in 1812. Though a military success, this campaign decimated the Great Army, causing the death of nearly a million soldiers and civilians. Plath only directly mentions the swarm in the fourth stanza, focusing on the man/Napoleon instead. She also compares bees to soldiers in the poem 'Wintering'. After several attacks from the man, the wild swarm disperses, but the bees congregate around the queen's hiding place in a tree. Like the French troops, 'The bees have got so far. Seventy feet high! / Russia, Poland and Germany!' Once again, the speaker points out their heroism by comparing them to French soldiers successfully crossing the Berezina river. The man is assaulting the bees again, and as true mutineers, they argue over the strategy to adopt to riot. Like Napoleon with his men, he is shattering their dreams and their destiny.

The battle is coming to an end: the swarm falls into a bush. The speaker pays their respects to the fallen bees: 'So much for the charioteers, the outriders, the Grand Army!' Yet they also praise the man: 'A red tatter, Napoleon!' Then 'The swarm is knocked into a cocked straw hat', a subtle reference to Napoleon's famous bicorne hat, an act that is 'The last badge of victory.' The defeated bees must retreat like Napoleon at Elba or die. The bees become 'marshals, admirals, generals / Worming themselves into niches', in other words they withdraw into their cells. Their whiteness recalls bee larvae.

The bodies of the bees are 'draped with Mother France's upholstery / Into a new mausoleum', a small consolation. Their persecutor is proud of himself, he displays 'The smile of a man of business, intensely practical.' His toxic attitude is revealed by the way Plath describes his hands: they are 'asbestos receptacles.' The man justifies his action with the line: '"They would have killed *me*."' Although his fear is not completely unfounded (bee stings only become fatal if they are numerous, but a single sting can lead to death by anaphylactic reaction with allergic people), the speaker mocks this man with a God-like complex. In his mind, the bees are cunning and fearful enemies that need to be beaten. Plath sarcastically writes: 'Napoleon is pleased, he is pleased with everything.' For her, this man's obsession with controlling nature and

---

[3] Fondation Napoléon, les-guerres-napoleoniennes_-combien-de-morts-_je_4-10-2022_revumb-1.pdf.

exterminating it when he cannot dominate it is a disgrace. Like Napoleon, he sees his 'fight' as an act of bravery and does not consider for one moment the bees' lives. They are only there to produce honey for his consumption, the way French soldiers only existed in Napoleon's mind as a tool to achieve glory. Plath concludes the poem with: 'O Europe! O ton of honey!', a metaphor for each man's ambition: a continent and a product. Napoleon's egotistical attitude was responsible for the death of millions of Europeans, whereas the man's persecution killed thousands of bees.

A lot has been written about Plath's use of World War II references throughout *Ariel* (famously in poems like 'Daddy' and 'Lady Lazarus'), but as 'The Swarm' demonstrates, she mentioned other European wars in her writing. Her five bee poems were written over the course of seven days, but 'The Swarm' clearly stands out because of its historical references and extended metaphor. The conflict between man and nature is at its peak here. Plath also explored the power dynamics between a head of state/the beekeeper and its people/the bees in 'The Arrival of the Bee Box', where she compared the bees to the Romans and herself to Caesar. Most of the time, she described human interactions with bees in terms of humility: in 'Wintering', the speaker crucially admits: 'It is they who own me.' 'The Bee Meeting' and 'Stings' depict the physical vulnerability of working with bees. And in 'The Swarm', Plath turned the bees into veterans and fallen heroes sacrificed for one man's megalomania to highlight that nature is a victim of humanity's sense of superiority.

Julie Irigaray

Reviews

Sue Wallace-Shaddad looks at a new collection, fresh as its yellow jacket cover.

Tormentil
Ian Humphreys
Nine Arches Press, £10.99

Nature, and in particular the healing plant 'tormentil', with its yellow flowers, appears repeatedly in the collection offering a sense of comfort in the background. The book is dedicated to the poet's mother, and the poem 'Rebirth' has a footnote explaining that the phrase 'One of 784' signifies she was one of that number who died in hospital from Covid-19. The poet writes poignantly 'I catch your colours/ in every living thing' and lists the 'bumble bee', 'moth', 'robin eggs' and 'mallards'.

The first poem 'Tormentil' opens with the line 'I can't face the big stuff', so the narrator searches for the 'gold thread' of the flower on the moors. The name 'tormentil' includes the word 'torment'. The plant appears again in the moving poem 'tormentil +' where the flowers are compared to 'a thousand compasses' but they are of no help when the narrator feels 'lost'. In 'Firecrest', a poem suffused with the colour yellow, the flowers are 'frail stars' and 'golden children'. There is even a poem, 'Mouse-ear Hawkweed', about a plant 'that isn't tormentil' but is yellow and also has healing properties.

Tormentil is also part of a 'lemon love posy for Judy' in 'Punch and Judy on the West Yorkshire Moors'. In this prose poem, Punch and Judy 'ghost-float above the tops, flapping in the wind'. Humphreys often utilises compound words. This can be particularly effective when the poem employs surrealism. In 'There's a walrus on my windscreen', the second line describes 'the bristle-blubber-blood of it'. The walrus has been 'digger-scooped' and 'then re-routed to a snowblitz'. This poem is a startling indictment of the way human beings are destroying the natural world. Other examples of compound words can be found in 'On spilling a jug of Mai Tai plus half a pale ale over the new marketing director's lap during her welcome drinks': 'double-ginned priest', 'fizz-bomb', 'sun-flared neck'. I particularly enjoyed the visual image created by the poet's use of 'dandruff' as a verb in the lines:

I dandruff down

to lightly season
our Head of HR's warm pear cider.

Humphreys packs this collection with a tremendous range of topics, including aspects of West Yorkshire and also the queer scene. The poet muses on the building of walls in the prose poem 'Walltown': 'They knew how to build walls in these parts'. The words 'private' and 'keep out' are repeated several times, emphasising the power of walls to 'hold back', though what they hold back may not be clear. 'The Rochdale Canal' with its 'painted narrow boats' is a poignant poem of reminiscence: 'On a picnic bench by The Stubbing Wharf, you slipped/ breaded scampi from your plate to mine'. 'The other lot' highlights social divide: they aim to 'keep our lot in our moleholes./ They mine darker pits for us to fall into.' He writes about drag queens and the international queer scene, reminding the reader of those victimised in 'Prayer for the Fabulous Ones'. Closer to home, 'Like a record, baby' suggests there is a risk '*we'll fall off the edge*'. 'Pansies' reflects on 'the old guard' with their 'Camp compliance/ trowelled thick as luvvie slap'.

A rich strand to the collection is that of cultural heritage. In 'Hak gwai', the reader learns that 'Mum emigrated at twenty'. In 'Lady Luck', the poet contrasts 'Mong Kok's leaning towers   of dim sum baskets' with 'In Hythe   boiled-cabbage streets steamed with winter breath'. A ward nurse is confused by the family's mixed heritage in 'Hak gwai'. Those two words, which mean 'black devil in Cantonese', also feature in the prose poem 'Whose Story?', which recounts a tale about the narrator's great-great-grandfather, a decorated soldier from Mozambique. However, the narrator comments, he

dreamt up most of this story
because my people's history
is spun on whispers.

'*But where do you really come from?*' has a list of possible ancestry with eighteen lines of percentages which don't add up to 100%, implying, perhaps, that one can never be sure of the ethnic mix one has inherited.

Humour is also employed to powerful effect in several poems. 'Paucity', written as two columns, plays on words beginning with the letter 'P'. It is an amusing take on the poetry world. The poem ends 'I love their energy   but we're not on the same page'. 'Refrain' tells of a group of twitchers waiting for the visiting bird's 'haunting mating call' but

Look at it
sitting there on that branch
being quiet.

The poem 'Grey Matter' which describes discouraging a squirrel, that 'Bushytailed boss man', by greasing the bird feeder pole also raised a smile.

Several nature poems are lyrical. The frequent alliteration of 's' in 'Cotton-grass, late spring' creates a gentle mood, for example, in the first stanza:

When tiredness drums,
lie down softly and
sift white clouds

'Morning Swim, 1979', paints a beautiful description of a water vole beside the river Dane: 'Those eyes – two drops/ of black rain – never leave mine'. Humphreys breaks his couplets to create a ripple effect at the centre of the poem. Another lyrical poem 'When trees burn', '*after Philip Larkin*', touches on loss with the lines 'Spring's beacon shines, disowning grief/ disarming winter's last-gasp gloom.' 'Falling galaxies', near the end of the collection, reads as a reconciliation with grief. When walking over 'the high moor', 'From nowhere, a voice within me/ blesses your name'.

There is much to savour in this collection, with its powerful sense of place and appreciation of the natural world. At its heart is an acknowledgement of heritage and coming to terms with loss.

Sue Wallace-Shaddad

Julian Bishop looks at two collections and a pamphlet that each offer different but distinctly unsettling views of the world.

Elisabeth Sennitt Clough
My Name is Abilene
Salt, £10.99

Emma Simon
Shapeshifting For Beginners
Salt, £10.99

Simon Maddrell
Isle of Sin
Polari, £8

Stylistically and thematically, Elisabeth Sennitt Clough's *My Name is Abilene* is the illegitimate child of Robin Robertson and Fiona Benson, a grimoire journey through abuse against the louring backdrop of the fens. Like Robertson's *The Long Take*, it's a poetic narrative, although delivered snapshot-like in the manner of Benson's *Zeus* poems. The poems are often untitled, divided only by a fleuron, appropriate given how flowers, plants – and in particular potatoes – feature in the collection.

The text is in lower case throughout, which has a levelling effect on some of the horror. Abeline's world is one emptied of meaning and hope but filled with shrill social media feeds, not dissimilar to her mother's:

> i think of mum three shots to the wind
> on the back kitchen floor
> empty bottles beneath potato peel
> brace sat with benny hill and a plate of greasy chips
> *she'll get up when she's ready* he mutters

Intergenerational abuse seeps through the book as abilene embarks on a relationship with bland but violent john, himself the victim of an abusive upbringing. The first part of the book builds towards what feels like an inevitable rape but it ends up being suppressed by euphemism and acronyms, as the powerful poem (note: with capitals) 'When I Talk About Codes' makes clear:

> There are two codes at the top of my medical record.

I see them each time I order a prescription.
These codes are immediately followed by their explanations:
X767N rape and XaEFu physical abuse.
This undermines the idea of codes as secret or indirect.

Secrecy finds a fertile home in the Fenlands setting. In 'paradise farm' Sennitt Clough paints a picture of countryside where 'the fen wind pants/ round the concrete floor' of a place called Paradise Farm and then goes 'out the doorway/ where it worries the asbestos roof' and a character called brace shoots foxes to string up on a tree. The poem ends:

he piles
foxes in the back of his motor to take to town, where
he sells them at the back door of a restaurant. now i
understand his laughter. i ask him the name of the place,
but he revs away to buy more cartridges

Razor endings like this keep up the narrative pace, again an echo of Benson's technique in *Zeus*. Occasionally I wonder if the technique (and the nihilism) is overplayed, a sentiment perhaps the poet is conscious of. Towards the end of the book, the poems (post relationship with john) are more reflective and nuanced. In 'it's about a small plot of land', abeline wonders whether 'we fen dwellers are what savage minds make us' and refers to a local radio broadcaster who created a fictional fenman:

i always felt uneasy the broadcaster said
in making his imaginary fen village *so squalid*
hopeless and all round awful
but i blame the public - savage is what they wanted
but now, john, they're not so sure

Sennitt Clough explains in an interview for the Forward Prize (her book was shortlisted for Best Collection 2023) that the name abilene came from putting her name into an anagram-maker and one of the phrases it threw out was 'abilene fluorescent nightclothes.' She adds: 'I challenged myself to write a poem from that prompt and the title poem of the collection was the result. At the time, I was going through some difficulties in my personal life. It was the year of lockdowns and I stepped into the persona of abilene. She became an imaginative extension of my life and personality.'

Our first proper introduction to the character comes a few pages in when we learn that 'the girl abilene/ is always there for songs and stories and to let you/ know your cabbage field's been set alight.' It's a good example of how wit and original imagery often save the poems from veering into a misery fest. Later in the book we learn she wears a lipstick called '*rouge999*' and later on that 'I plant myself in a clunchy field/ like a potato':

> when you buy a potato it's still living
> no heart no pulse but all of its potato
> family instinctively know it as a conscious being
> she asks how i'm getting on
> and i say *like a potato, sis,*
> *like a potato*

The poems are divided into two sections, 'before john' and 'abilene' and tellingly the latter section uses john's viewpoint as a lens rather than abilene's, hence perhaps the presence of a poem entitled 'in the town of the gaslit women' where the roads out of town 'hiss and froth'. It comes as no surprise to find out in 'what john said' that he's as damaged as abilene:

> my mother had a millefiori paperweight
> i carry its impact
> at the corner of my lip
> where it dozes
> like a shiny bloodsucker

Ultimately, there are no happy endings here, just a tatty receipt containing 'one fizzing fly on life's carcass'.

***

It's quite hard to get a handle on Emma Simon's debut collection *Shapeshifting For Beginners* but actually I guess that's the point. Simon's range is wide and wild, shifting from a sequence about Grandma Frankenstein to a tender poem about swallows in just a couple of pages. What unites these poems though is the poet's ability to conjure majesty, magic and weirdness out of the relatively mundane.

Take the aforementioned swallows. The poem's actually called 'Swallows Rest Home' where the birds are 'perched in wing-back chairs, staring/ as sky rolls through day-room windows.' The birds are 'nested in pillows, earthbound, bedsore' and it's not too difficult to see the poem as a clever reverse metaphor.

The ghost of Robert Browning's 'My Last Duchess' looms large, as indeed it might in any collection where the poet adopts multiple identities. One poem called 'Bad Feminists', with a pleasing end-rhyme scheme, pays explicit tribute to him, although here the portrait is a naked David Beckham:

> Caught on film,
> spooled day and night inside this darkened room
> for us selected few – the women who appreciate
> a perfect nude, swathed in Egyptian cotton sheets.
> Though quite untouchable. Still, it works both ways.

It's a good example of how Simon's imagination is allowed to run wonderfully riot. With some poems, I wondered which came first, the title or content, particularly when they read like a poetry challenge. Take 'My Life as a B-List Movie Star' where the poet throws herself into the role with relish:

> You can flash them your best fifty-foot smile,
> Don, Dan or Sam or whoever else is manfully
>
> making his way to the rescue. Eyes all the same,
> bright pockets of sky, whose laser-like glares
> fail to pierce the dark heart of your problems.

The poem incorporates another element that runs through the collection, a sardonic wit aimed variously at those in authority and men (which of course often amounts to much the same thing).

Continuing in the vein of eye-catching titles, 'Poem that is haunted by the ghost of my mother, singing, and a fleeting after-image of Emily Dickinson' is almost a poem in itself, but the poet immediately undercuts any assumptions of showboating by beginning

> Another one, if I'm honest. Sometimes I put my ear
> to the page to make out the words –
> but it's just that trapped fly buzzing of my brain.

A way of saying this is me, there's no posturing going on here. I like the attention paid to the end words here: ear, words, brain, the three working in harmony throughout the collection. The poem's about the process of converting thoughts and feeling into words, the poetic process itself. It ends:

Luxuriate here instead, in all this white space,
enjoying the lemon spritz, swish of summer breeze
through plane trees, or whatever else this poem

or the next might be about. Come on,
don't tell me you can't hear her, now and again,
singing slightly out of tune.

The tone of the poems veers between the confident and self-critical but any heaviness is levitated by the wit. In 'A Mermaid's Complaint' (to her therapist) she considers her 'mutinous' legs:

A man described them as a sturdy set of pins
and he was right: like upturned skittles,
waiting to be bowled over.

But the poem ends on a triumphant note, concluding they're covered in sequins 'hard as silver fish scales'. There's similar relish in a poem called 'The Derry Street Trials', which references the Witch trials of the 17th century and today, where women are subject to the same unwinnable trials in the tabloid press:

If she has no children. Or too many.
Leaves them a-bed while she slips out to conjure coins from the beamy air,

or stays at home, bricked behind her walls
without a man to breathe life in her fire, then she's a witch

Witches, monsters, poltergeists and the Gothic rampage through the collection but so do Bagpuss, a White Blancmange Rabbit and a pile of washing. There's a 'Pindaric Ode to Robert Smith' of the Cure which becomes a wistful look-back to youth's 'hairspray fog' of 'wonky posters' in bedrooms and 'all that wasted heartache'. At a Cure reunion gig where Smith (and presumably the poet) still peddles 'a wry belipsticked smile' she concludes 'Nothing has altered. It all remains the same.'

***

Simon Maddrell's chapbook *Isle Of Sin* is an excoriating account of institutionalised homophobia and prejudice on the Isle of Man, where he was born. The poems are dedicated to gay rights activist Alan Shea who fought – and won – a campaign for the legalisation of sex between men and a subsequent apology from the police.

Maddrell seeks to expose the vindictiveness and hypocrisy at work that prevented the law being changed on what he calls 'this sexsick island', taking aim at the police, Manx Parliament and a cast of homophobes. The first few poems consider the life and legacy of actor Dursley McLinden, who died of AIDS in 1995 and helped inspire the character of Ritchie in the C4 drama *It's A Sin*. A powerful opening sonnet 'Bells & Bells' concludes:

> Not all bells were quelled after yours
> too many other graves left unmarked
> or planted with trees hiding their
> truth instead of friends surrounding
> them when the soil was fresh & ready

The pamphlet then broadens out to take a more political tack, satirising an anti-gay campaigner who

> clings to his pineapples
> and palms their stone column
> as if his whole masculinity
> depended upon them

The cast of characters is extensive for a small pamphlet and what Maddrell calls 'Notes & Queeries' possibly contain more words than the poems themselves. I wonder if a single-page introduction at the front might have saved constant flicking to the back? The research however is admirably extensive. Four of the poems are erasure poems, the most effective one the belated and mealy-mouthed apology from the Chief Constable:

> Police officers ~~cannot~~ choose which laws' to enforce they ~~cannot~~ have an opinion on the rightness or virtue of legislation, and they ~~must not~~ allow their personal opinions to affect how they work

However, another erasure from an Isle of Man Government statement, while important, lacks the same impact, which raises the issue of editing. I felt some poems could have been pushed more, for example 'Life Was A Trapdoor' mentions six types of trapdoor in five stanzas; it begs to be six.

But these are small quibbles. For a small pamphlet, it packs a mighty punch and as Peter Tatchell reminds us in an endorsement, it's 'a stark reminder of where we came from and where we could return'.

Julian Bishop

SK Grout reviews three collections that explore performance and language, through poetry, history and algorithms, and the implications for the body.

Jason Allen-Paisant
Self-Portrait as Othello
Carcanet Poetry, £12.99

Mary Jean Chan
Bright Fear
Faber, £10.99

Ellora Sutton
Artisanal Slush
Verve Poetry Press, £7.99

'Who lives, who dies, who tells your story', the most famous refrain from the musical *Hamilton*, examines who is apportioned the role of history's winners and losers, how and why we remember what we do. Jason Allen-Paisant's Forward Prizewinning, PBS Choice and second collection *Self-Portrait as Othello* is a collection which explores narrative from all angles, how a story is told and who becomes the main character through this telling. Allen-Paisant disrupts time and space, and asks what may be left behind, and/or what stands outside the frame.

Narrative is the poetic device propelling the first section. A number of vignettes are told from the speaker's perspective, possibly autobiographical, potentially a version of the titular Othello reimagined as a traveller-student from the Caribbean to Europe. 'I am five. I sit at the barbecue' opens the nearly twenty pages of untitled verse; we are told a barbecue is a stone structure used to dry coffee in Jamaica.

These poems move through time and space – Jamaica, Paris, Prague, Venice, Munich, Oxford – and mix languages – French, English, German, Italian and patois, for example on page 35: 'Watch me speaking four languages outside the club.', and again on page 26:

> the sound of pain is a winding whining
>   *dou dou douleur doudou* dance wid me
> is a wine in my mouth is a sexiness of the words

Time is not linear, it swirls and changes direction to serve the narrative rather than record events. The opening poem of the collection, 'Ringing Othello', ends: 'I conjure you / furiously'. The verb is mystical and old: suggests bringing someone back, the line between the living and dead is porous, what's imagined, what's real, that memory lives in the body. We are reminded of Othello, but we become attuned to the sporadic presence of 'daddy', of 'Un-Dad' in these early pages (evoking the half rhyme undead). Like Othello, this figure grows large in the consciousness and becomes neither dead nor alive, but present through memory. 'I'm haunted as much by the character Othello as by the silences in the story' ('Self-Portrait as Othello I'). This culminates in the poem 'Othello Walks' where he is reimagined walking through Venice yet 'his skin betrays him'. The second half concludes

> you're following your father's
>
> footsteps across the oceans.
> You're looking for him in the wind.

Indeed, Section Three is a moving meditation on grief and how it presents itself in the public and private sphere. 'I look for Mama's voice in Dropbox' ('To Find Mama's Voice'). The penultimate poem 'Door of No Return' (named after a quote from Dionne Brand) considers names and naming: 'I took the name *Paisant*' and 'In Paris, I met a man by the name of Richard Allen'. Ultimately, as in the first poem, it explores how to communicate across the barrier of loss. 'My father, I address you, as you crouch/ in the dark corner'.

The second section engages with ekphrasis, history and form and several poems are titled 'Self-Portrait as Othello'. '*Stories* are everything/ for my audience' ('Self-Portrait as Othello IV'). Some poems re-imagine his backstory as in 'Othello Walks' while others evoke Desdemona and speak to the history of the slave trade in Italy and wider Europe. From 'Who Is Othello? II':

> The decree of 1489 distinguished
> between white and black slaves
> for the first time

'Self-Portrait as Othello I' moves through the play 'Iago the language' and history 'When he wrote *Othello*, the slave trade had been happening for seven decades, with the Pope's blessing'. The poem quotes from the play *even now very now*

an old black ram is
tupping your white ewe

and remains in the present tense when addressing the reader

and still – dare I believe

that I was no fetish, that this
my body was real to you?

What remains memorable in these poems is the impression of the body. From the moving poem 'Place de la Nation', dedicated to Ahmaud Arbery:

The crowd must be thick
or you will see your body

raising suspicions by walking
you do not want that

'There are Moor heads everywhere. We're not talking about this.' we are told in the poem 'The Picture and the Frame' which acts as a kind of organising principle for the collection as it moves through its themes and preoccupations in a long zuihitsu format. The poem speaks to the gaps in language and the spaces they create, and as the title suggests, urges us to consider what may be omitted or left outside the (white) gaze. 'The Moor remains invisible, despite the obsession with his body.'

Édouard Glissant wrote of '...one who is errant (who is no longer traveler, discoverer, or conqueror) strives to know the totality of the world yet already knows he will never accomplish this – and knows that is precisely where the threatened beauty of the world resides.'[4] This is an apt description for Othello, a character evoked in the play through his body rather than his life and story, and Allen-Paisant moves through borders and limits of time, place, death and the body to engage with story-

[4] Édouard Glissant, *Poetics of Relation*, translated by Betsy Wing, the University of Michigan Press, 1997.

telling. From 'The Picture and the Frame': 'Nothing makes sense until it makes sense in the body, till the body is present at the making-sense.'

***

Mary Jean Chan's Forward Prize nominated, PBS Recommendation and second collection, *Bright Fear* explores what it means to be tender in the face of adversity, and how a poem can translate the body and its experiences, its placement on the page and its engagement with language.

The collection is divided into three sections, 'Grief Lessons', 'Ars Poetica' and 'Field Notes on a Family' with two single poems book-ending the collection. Each section holds its own space, nuanced alterations are made to voice, tone and formal inquiries about what a poem can do, speaking to the topics of grief, poetry and family. Still there are echoes and idea-relays that connect across poems. In each section, the poems explore what language as a performance looks and sounds like, either as the speaker performs or language is performed around them; some poems are intimate and discrete, others range across time and space.

The first section uses language that is more straightforward, less prone to metaphor, and metaphoric leaps as in the third section, 'there is too much language, / too little time' ('Bright Fear I') versus 'Her mouth was a gate / you unbolted' ('Glance'). The tone is more direct, and perhaps this is because of subject matter; Chan suggests to us that topics such as micro-aggressions, racism, queerphobia, the pandemic and grief require language that doesn't obfuscate or circle around a point. From 'Answer'

> At the Poetry Café, some-
>   one sipping tea once stared
>   at me from across the room
>
> and asked, are you a man or
>   a woman? I want to know too.

The poems engage with mortality – both the recent Covid-19 pandemic and the SARS epidemic ('At thirteen, school meant mandatory/ medical kits' ('Hong Kong, 2003') – and how we negotiate space. 'What does it mean to want to live?' ('Love for the Living'). Two poems have the same title as the collection, and three poems use the title 'EDI for Migrants'. This acronym is solved in the final line of the third poem – 'Equality Diversity Inclusion' – and all three situate themselves in public spaces: an online conference, a cultural awareness event and an airplane.

A search tells me EDI also stands for Electronic Data Interchange (where paper communication has been superseded by the electronic, for example invoices) and this meaning-trace hovers over a number of poems taking place in online spaces, necessitated by the pandemic but also speaking to those separated by space and time, by differing government lockdown policies.

The second section – 'Ars Poetica' – is one long poem broken into sixteen sections; or perhaps it is sixteen poems given connected titles of Roman numerals. The first poem almost sets itself as manifesto, as an engagement with the concept of hybridity, of fluidity, of avoiding what is pinned down and categorised. 'The poet opened a clean Word document, titled it *POETRY*, then saved it in a folder titled *NONFICTION*, then saved it in a folder titled *FICTION*.' 'XIV' is a prose poem, yet each sentence engages with the fragmentary and multi-vocal, quoting Sara Ahmed, Billy-Ray Belcourt and José Esteban Muñoz. The poem's ideas connect to each other by meaning formed by the whole, describing, 'In a poem about postcolonial grief, the speaker remains queer.' There is hybridity across the collection; even 'Sestina' from 'Grief Lessons' contains the kind of driving, compulsive reading experience often found in prose, and several poems engage with the white space inside a poem ('imperfection's school' and 'Glance'). Each of the poems in this section reckon with the way poetry can imagine and create the world anew for the speaker, the reader and the poet. From 'XVI'

> Perhaps
> here is home, in the long poem
> of our lives.

Section three contains poems about family. These are poems about sharing space, intimacy such as food as metaphor for love, but also about how the political and historical impact the personal. 'History must suffice. / My mother knew hunger.' ('Hindsight'). Chan engages with these ideas in a number of earlier poems ('my poetry students don't know/ they've saved me', 'XII'), and indeed each section both amplifies previous poems, as well as bringing these subjects into sharp relief. 'Write something cheerful, you and Dad urged, as if poetry were comedy.' ('A Denim Shirt'). These are intimate poems that discuss wide ranging topics, and take place in locations around the world, and in-between spaces ('In this city I am ahead of time' ('After Twenty-One Days in Hotel Quarantine')) and negotiate with something that defies fixity. Family is often, though not always, comprised of people who know us best, through proximity or longevity; yet family is a paradox. We keep our deepest secrets often from those who know us best. From 'How It Must Be Said': 'Do you want to be liked or seen? My therapist asks. Each year, I migrate between cities and selves. How a familiar voice can make one weep.'

The second section acts as a kind of hinge, both for the contours of a book, but also between the subjects of grief and family. In this way, Chan suggests poetry acts as a hinge between these two large subjects. Their poetry is personal and often about family, or grief borne of the not-quite, but perhaps the work of their life is to write into a space 'language no longer meaning / rift or sorrow but its opposite' ('The Translator').

***

Ellora Sutton's third pamphlet, *Artisanal Slush*, is an exploration of the self through online spaces such as fandom and AI. It also asks the questions – what preoccupies you? What do you spend your time on? What brings you joy?

Each poem is an exploration of time, archiving the present moment and cataloguing experience as a museum piece that collides the past and the future into the now. 'Its like being lost in IKEA. How it all gets very multi-burial very quickly' ('Archaeology Phrasebook') and 'For I too play *Tetris* on company time' ('I think I might be Dennis Nedry').

These museum pieces are made up of what it means to be alive in the 2020s; Lisa Simpson, My Chemical Romance, Coca-Cola vs Pepsi, Taylor Swift, cottagecore, *Doctor Who* are all featured. These are poems that engage with online spaces in their content – fanfiction, *The Sims,* alternative universes, Urban Dictionary – but also with their form. 'My computer thinks I'm gay' is co-written with AI. Sutton includes a cento titled 'Self-Portrait as Facebook Ads' and a number of poems include final lines such as '[New password must be different from old password]' or '[loading … loading]' suggesting the multi-dimensional space of a screen; that by a click of a button or a scroll of a mouse one can be taken elsewhere in seconds.

Sutton wears her influences on her sleeve – 'the many five star reviews of my performance / in the dual role of Courtney Love/John Keats' ('In a field on a clear night, I might say') – and draws inspiration from far and wide. A number of poems were written during a residency at Petersfield Museum and Art Gallery and another poem is addressed to Tom Nook, a character from *Animal Crossing.* Even the twelfth century mystic Hildegard von Bingen makes an appearance.

What remains consistent is Sutton's voice, drawing the reader in tenderly and conspiratorially, as if sharing a secret or dream. These poems deserve a soft epilogue[5] and reach for the intimacy between speaker and reader through what it means to be alive and seeking joy in the modern world.

SK Grout

[5] 'We deserve a soft epilogue, my love' is a famous title of a fanfiction story depicting Steve Rogers and James Buchanan 'Bucky' Barnes of the MCU. https://fanlore.org/wiki/We_deserve_a_soft_epilogue,_my_love

Lesley Sharpe considers acts of recalibration in a prizewinning debut pamphlet.

Serena Alagappan
Sensitive to Temperature
Smith|Doorstop, £6

Serena Alagappan's first pamphlet, *Sensitive to Temperature*, which won The Poetry Business 2022 New Poets Prize, considers the personal and wider implications of change, with temperature as barometer for everything that shifts beyond the poet's control. Positioning the close detail of individual lives within the wider scope of an inscrutable universe, Alagappan incorporates the movements of both ecosystems and planetary orbits, their influence 'as certain as the globe/ warming, fake medicine, false starts, real healing' ('Clockwork').

This contradictory sense of proximity and distance energises Alagappan's poems, as in 'Let's Catch Up Soon', which attempts to 'ventriloquize/ that leaf, or the veins bulging/ inside it', while opening a broader metaphor:

> Waiting for fruits to soften
> is waiting for a friend
> with whom it's been a long
> time since you've spoken.

Sensitivity to time as well as temperature is evident, where perception animates 'indiscernibly small and precise recalibrations' ('Clockwork'): 'We blink and the world rearranges./ We blink and it remains unchanged.'

In addition to the tiny shifts of behaviour in which the slightest adjustment of temperature implies a radical recalibration of experience – temperature as mood, as health, as intimate participant in the process that initiates decay – there are the movements of deep time, planets, the formation of rivers. Spare, encyclopaedic in tone,

> One orbit, which lasts 405,000 years,
> helps geologists measure planetary
> dynamics

while elsewhere, Alagappan's explorations with poetic form shape the fluid structure of 'The Beginning of the Thames', which weaves its way across the page to create a small river of space:

> if a river   can begin this clear, then low
> hours can climb their way   out new mouths.

Amid the languid tone is characteristic compression of imagery, where a

> Seaweed storm
> below surface glass permits a green   reflection   green, as in
> newly alive, chlorophyll- innocence.

This sense of the pristine, pitted against immanent loss, appears in 'Aurora', where 'ignorance is   both a blessing   and a curse', and the poet reveals

> Everything   became
> slippery   confusing   after the first

In this way, questions of perspective and scale lie at the heart of the sequence, its title poem 'Sensitive to Temperature' imagining icicles on a satellite of Jupiter, whose

> frigid mountain vanes are just a few hundred million miles
> away. They live close too: in me and you, sensitive to temperature,
> frozen in numb rapture.

With all distance undercut by the simple word 'just', that 'numb rapture' might explode its potential. Again, Alagappan yokes unexpected images in 'How Dark the Beginning', as the speaker realises 'My tee-shirt mapped a constellation of stars'. In 'Red Moon', another closeness prevents perception: 'your hand was not only /too close to see, but also preventing your sight'. Powerful compressions attempt to resolve contradiction: 'there is not one heart for love and/ one for hatred. There is only one heart for both.'

Moments of crisis balance acts of regeneration, sometimes strange and unsettling, as in 'After the Mushroom at the End of the World', a poem whose scale is simultaneously monumental and minute to picture 'how after nuclear disaster/ mushrooms grow on reactor walls'. Imitating the life-giving process by 'harnessing radiation like purple/

alliums photosynthesize light', they are even, the speaker concludes, 'sucking energy from decay' in vampiric acts of self-renewal.

How far might these poetic acts of recognition become aesthetic remedies, as urgent as the opening poem 'slipface', whose sensitivities seem time-critical, and the poet asks, 'has the moment passed'? In the sparks of fire 'aestheticized, / anthropomorphised' as 'giddy stars' in 'Forest Fire from Far Away', the poet makes explicit an anthropomorphism which projects everything in its own image, chief destroyer cast also as chief creator, to ask what the earth, with its 'bloodshot sea', will 'bear/ for this brutality?' Similarly, in 'The Sky Has a Body', the sickness of the natural world is humanised to engage our attention: 'The sky runs a fever', and 'wheezes with its wind', till finally, impossible to ignore, it 'weeps from every pore'.

Amid this uncertainty, the poet dives deep to unearth, in acts of anaphora, a redeeming sense of the sacred, declaring

> Holy the indigo aura
> that casts doubt on a landscape's
> verity. Fog or foam, snow caps or sea?

Ambiguity and destruction contain the holistic elements of rebirth, aligned with deeper cycles of time:

> Holy the volcano, and
> the ones spared
> from the volcano,
> and the volcano's fertile sand.

These are poems of beginnings and endings, and of the strange middle ground between. Alagappan's enquiry investigates this territory in accomplished poems that prove that 'everything we can see can shrink/ or magnify, meaning, sight is plastic' ('Clockwork'). Memory and imagination also become tools of navigation, distinctively human attributes which are elusive, but essential, to meet and anticipate change on whatever scale, for 'the past you can't remember is the future you can't imagine' ('The Body Keeps the Score').

Lesley Sharpe

Tamsin Hopkins enjoys an accomplished first collection, discovers the emotional impact of local landscape around the River Stour and gets physical with an A4 collection.

Yvonne Reddick
Burning Season
Bloodaxe Books, £10.99

Emily Hasler
Local Interest
Pavilion Poetry, Liverpool University Press, £8.80

Briony Hughes
Rhizomes
Broken Sleep Books, £24.99

Although this is Yvonne Reddick's first full collection, she has previously published four pamphlets, including *Translating Mountains* (Seren, 2017) which won the *Mslexia* Women's Pamphlet Competition. In *Burning Season* she continues to expand her ecopoetry practice with poems of loss and profound personal grief for a father who worked on oil rigs, loved hiking and bequeathed a love of the natural world and the mountains to his daughter.

Reddick's poems are alive with birds, trees, plants, mountains and water. A particular strength of the collection is the consistent naming of landscape and geography with an alertness to evocative, sonic qualities. Even the oil fields and types of oil are named: 'Galahad', 'Ravenspurn', 'Ekofisk', and 'Bonny Light' and 'Sour heavy Crude'. Reddick also employs the gorgeous names of lakes and mountains ('Shiehallion,' 'Madness Lake,' 'Spitzen,' 'Corni'). In 'Translating Mountains from the Gaelic' we are given *'Beinn Laoghail', 'Beinn Uais'* and *'Bod an Deamhain'*. The speaker in the poems always pays attention to the physicality of the natural world, placing the reader in that environment with a deft touch born of lived experience. In 'The Flower that Breaks Rock', snow saxifrage is 'Dainty Alpinist, chinking her roots into fissures/ and fractures, like crampons in toeholds.'

Woven through loss, war, family poems and polyvocal pieces in dramatic form, is a thread of short diary-like entries which serve as handholds for the reader to follow the speaker's movement forward through the trouble. These prose pieces act as islands of peace and hope. They are given months of the year as titles and chart the growth of acorns the speaker has collected and planted. It is perhaps in these sections that the speaker is seen less as daughter, raconteur or mountaineer, and more as adult woman. She nurtures the acorns through the months as a mother might look after growing embryos. She is 'anxious mother of seedlings' ('November') and elsewhere, talking of other seedlings 'You trees are the only children I can bear/ to watch growing tall.' ('Fire-seed').

The title poem of this collection gained third place in the Gingko Prize for Ecopoetry 2022. 'Burning Season' is a moving account of loss. Autumn leaves and bonfires which yield images of the father in smoke are contrasted with the images of him tending to oleanders and date palms, recalling when he worked in the oil industry in the Middle East.

In places the writing is urgent, as ecopoetry must be. Reddick describes the natural world with masterful attention to detail:

> Even their eyelids are feathered.
> The most High Artic of British birds,
> that cry like the clacking of pebbles. ('Ptarmigan')

Thinking about the collection as a whole, 'Rime' was one of my favourite poems, although 'Waterland' – the musical long poem which concludes the collection was a close second.

> Barbed wire muffled by frost,
> snow snuffing light of out-of-season gorse.
>
> Grass on the spine of Skiddaw hardens
> to plumes, as if shed by swans
>
> following the Pole Star. ('Rime')

I find myself most transported by Reddick's more tightly controlled poems. For me it is in these that she shows her superb skills of observation.

***

In her second collection, Emily Hasler focusses on the shifting geography of the River Stour, located on the Suffolk-Essex borders. The concern here is to highlight how a relationship with place is necessarily reciprocal and participatory;[6] that humans are changed by their natural environment as much as they impress change on a specific landscape.

Poems are drawn from observations as a resident, as a keen birdwatcher and from her interest in local history. Much of this was researched in local libraries, and the poems often arise from intertextual relationships with 'a great many books' ('Notes'). The language is innovative, and the forms which result from this process are various, and include collage ('Suffolk Girls'), hybrids – in places leaning towards micro-fiction ('Defences') and riffs ('At Cobold Point'). Perhaps because the speaker's voice, or voices, necessarily become diverse, or at least more akin to fractals from using this practice intertextuality, this collection is less emotionally focussed than her first collection, *The Built Environment* (also from Pavilion), which was praised for its emotional concentration.

In interview, Hasler has said that her practice in writing this book grew from researching individual poems, into 'a wider practice: to dwell.[...] To inhabit rather than capture.'[1] As a result, the first poem ('A Mud') might be the textbook-perfect opening poem. It performs exactly that act of dwelling or inhabiting Hasler aims for, while being invitational, innovative (its subject matter is the co-mingling of mud and tidal seawater) and representative of the body of poems as a whole.

Some poems tend more towards the overtly political. These have more emotional force for me. In 'Black Tern' the speaker muses on hope and grief after a cold and wet birdwatching foray:

> This climate could be perfect,
> we wouldn't lose a single species
> but still the new ones would come:
> White-tailed eagle, Great auk, every tern.

I cannot decide which poem is my favourite – the opening poem or the final one, 'Goosefoot'. This last is simultaneously a love poem, an annotation of birdwatching and an illustration of (benign) obsession – an entirely effective and affective combination. The personal, the emotional and the external are woven through the poem across time, memory and sensory experience whilst being rooted in location. Repetition of the

---

[6] https://liverpooluniversitypress.blog/2023/03/14/local-interest-an-interview-with-emily-hasler/

phrase 'patte d'oie' (French for 'goosefoot'), the English word 'goosefoot' and a three-footed web symbol between stanzas make this concrete. Ending with a poem on a deeper emotional register is a satisfying and skilful way to summarise and bring this collection to a close.

***

Briony Hughes seeds the open spaces of the page with tight poems of witness and careful attention. Some were written in lockdown and record the emotional impact of that time on the landscape, including a fire on a golf course which devasted local ecology. Others are less easy to locate in space and time. Commissioned by Broken Sleep, *Rhizomes* consists of five sections, including *RHIZOME or TAPROOT,* which was previously published separately.[7]

Section one circles the natural disaster caused by the fire in a tone which could be employed equally in memoir, poetry or fiction. Using the third person, Hughes manages to express grief and tenderness by successfully merging trauma on three levels – the wild or of nature, the personal and the universal human level.

> we noticed that the trees had been chopped and it felt like a
> straightforward metaphor they said it would stop the flames from
> jumping so we agreed on a distance between trees and trenches
> near the road and the
>
> but how many times have you heard this story
>
> 01/09/2020

Along the long side of page 20, she follows this with: '*metaphor between trees and trenches*'.

The book is printed in A4 and has soft covers causing it to be flexible and tactile in the hand. The poems also encourage a physical engagement with the book as artefact since, in places, the reader has to turn it in different directions in order to chase syntax and find associations between the often disordered words. Section two has colour poems which

---

[7] *RHIZOME or TAPROOT* was originally collected in *Rewilding: An Ecopoetry Anthology* in 2020 and printed separately as a pamphlet by Paper View Books in 2022.

circle and build up like wasps gathering, which cause the reader to hold and turn the book as dictated by the poems. In other places, typographical choices such as the unusual deployment of parentheses and punctuation disrupt a conventional reading pattern. Section four consists of highly compressed poems presented as footnotes to blank pages, inviting the reader to participate and contribute by imagining and potentially adding content into the empty spaces.

Hughes's work uses simple, straight-talking language which accumulates emotion, becoming progressively more moving as the reader enters her world. She is particularly good at expressing how hard it is to communicate the emotions brought up by eco-grief.

> some of us wrote about how it was all fucked and tried to stamp the
> echo of a scream on the page
> but the mimicry of attempt
> could not resonate beyond our fingers.

Hughes's style employs little heightened or figurative language, although to say metaphors run deep in this collection is in keeping with the central emblem and the title. For non-gardeners, a rhizome runs horizontally just under the surface of the earth and produces new roots as side shoots. Ginger and Irises are good examples. If rhizomes have an opposing inclination in the plant world, it is the taproot – taproots run straight down into the earth, vertically seeking out nourishment with single purpose. *Rhizome* leaves a lasting impression of something communicated, something emotional and intangible having taken root in the mind, although the subtlety of the poems leaves this reader unsure of which way in her it will grow.

Tamsin Hopkins

Diana Cant looks at a debut collection that is a sustained elegy using a dazzling variety of forms, and a third collection in which the poet is troubled about the earth and our capacity to nurture it.

Paul Stephenson
Hard Drive
Carcanet Poetry, £12.99

David Clarke
The Field in Winter
Nine Arches Press, £10.99

I imagine this is not the debut collection Paul Stephenson originally intended to write. Stephenson's previous pamphlet, *Selfie with Waterlilies,* was published in 2017, and 'long-awaited' has been an epithet used in several reviews of this stunning collection. 'Long-awaited', we learn, for a compelling reason – the poet's long-standing partner died unexpectedly six years ago, and these poems are an extended elegy for him and for their relationship. They are also an exploration of grief and of the ways of surviving bereavement and loss – the ordinary and the extra-ordinary ways we have of keeping on keeping on.

On offer is a masterclass in writing and playing with form – and the poems are playful and humorous as well as brave, heart-stoppingly sad, and sure-footedly accomplished. In a book of over eighty poems, Stephenson manages to bring fresh forms to the celebration of a life lived with another. This is the poetry of witness, when the act of witnessing is active rather than passive, and creative rather than generic.

The poems form a narrative and are divided into six sections; the first three focus on a death and its immediate aftermath, the fourth and fifth are full of reflections on past, shared events, while the sixth pans out to the act of writing about a death and the ethical dilemmas involved. The collection is satisfyingly bookended by two poems, 'Anglepoise' and 'Wedding in Limousin'. The first is a quotidian description of two writers working companionably together in separate rooms, but with what we will come to recognise as a characteristic jolt at the end:

> We'll both be at home,
> absorbed in our projects,
> each working our way

through a bottle of red.
I'll be alive. You'll be alive.
It'll be like old times.

The reader is immediately plunged into the intimation that 'something is wrong' – the repetition of that phrase, and the sentence 'I had to see a student' ('The Thesis') is edgy, unsettling; all the lines are end-stopped, uncomfortable. It is followed by the shortest poem in the book, 'What Jean Saw', both shocking and devastating in its simplicity:

Through the letterbox
the little bald patch of you
asleep on the floor.

Details of the death are gradually and gracefully revealed; the questions we, as readers, want to ask are answered, but often a little after we have formulated them to ourselves – we are made to wait, as presumably was the poet. We are given a description of the mortuary, we witness a tender but unflinching description of viewing the body ('Signature'):

and with my thumb caress each fine brow,
stroke them in the right direction, feel the love
cold and wet from refrigeration.

Several poems go hand in hand with each other, for example, 'Your Name', which is a list poem of all the meanings of the word Tod, is followed by 'Conddolences', a riff on all the misspellings of Tod with a double 'd', in which words with two 'd's riddle through the poem. These last constitute a fine example of the sort of play with words and forms in which Stephenson excels.

The second section, to use Stephenson's own comment, is something of a 'soap-opera of accumulated characters', fondly rendered. There is Sarah from the funeral directors, Jade from the storage units, Michael the celebrant. In 'The Button', the poet movingly describes the awful ambivalence of the funeral, and the finality of pushing the crematorium button. And in 'Collecting You from Golders Green', Stephenson's formal inventiveness is used precisely to display the impossibility of finding the right words for any of this:

The young woman/lady/female
behind the desk/counter/reception
spoke gently/softly/calmly
  seemed genuinely moved/emotional/upset

There is a flat to be cleared, ashes to be scattered, 'stuff' to be dealt with. We ricochet from form to inventive form, perhaps in the way the mind zigzags from thought to thought, but always with the same underlying preoccupation. Stephenson has spoken about a quality of self-indulgence in grief, but perhaps self-absorption might be a kinder term.

In sections IV and V we move backwards in time – there are poems about shared journeys, meals, the intimate moments of an everyday life. Memory and grief draw the poet down internet rabbit holes in search of information about Birkenstocks and Justin Bieber. But there is a subtle shift in tenor; the poems, while still tender and personal, have the feeling of a balance tipping – there is a present; and although the past grief may intrude into the present, it is welcome, if unpredictable.

The final section addresses the validity of 'curating' a death. There is a movement away from the rawness of emotion; some of the immediacy has been replaced, not only by distance, but by an increased use of innovative form. This, I imagine was a purposeful, and emotionally accurate rendition of the process of grieving, yet there is a poignancy, and, for this reviewer, a relief in the return to the elegant simplicity and directness of the final, bookended poem, 'Wedding in Limousin':

All this way. I have come to represent you

but I'm also here for me. Hey, a swallow
just skimmed the pool, was off again.
Sixth in a row. A swallow for each year
you've been gone. It's time to swim.

Elizabeth Kubler-Ross, in her seminal work on grief and grieving says: 'The reality is that you will grieve for ever… You will be whole again, but you will never be the same. Nor should you be the same, nor would you want to.'[1] Paul Stephenson has given us a remarkable poetic demonstration of that truth in a work that is serious without being sombre, and is both playful and profound. I urge you to read it.

---

[1] Elizabeth Kubler-Ross, *The Gift of Grief, On Grief and Grieving* (Simon & Schuster, 2005)

***

David Clarke's third collection is primarily rooted in the natural landscape, often, and certainly initially, with an air of foreboding about the future of our planet. The poet worries for the earth – or rather, he worries about our capacity for 'dormant mischief that will wreck the world' ('A Spider in My Kitchen').

The poetic voice in the first part of the collection is lyrical and solitary – there is beauty, certainly, but little joy. A description of plums as 'drab sacks of skins' precedes the question 'Is summer still inside?' ('After the Plum Harvest'). It is a question to which he will return. Clarke's imagery is often alive with a prescience of death and all its symbolic heft ('Flies'):

> Such intricate corpses –
> they rustled on the sill in drifts,
> bludgeoned by their own wrong-headed
> butting at the windows,

or 'the bones/of people are kindling now,/ dry as bones that brute boys snap' ('Before Storm Ellen Arrives'). There is the bleakness of edgelands, and a vivid sense of desolation and despair, 'fly-tipped mattresses' and cows with 'woeful heads', while 'a pink sock flaps in razor wire' ('Fen Lane').

Not all the imagery is as bleak – 'tiny frogs// scatter and bounce like silver change' ('The Path from Krasnogruda to Ogrodniki'); starlings are 'Wideboys in from nowhere, they strut// in tonic suits' ('Starlings in the Garden'); a cobweb is 'fine as cattle-breath in frost' ('A Spider's Web on Exmoor').

Clarke's preferred poetic form is the sonnet – over half the poems in this collection are sonnets, mostly written with a 4/4/4/2 line structure. And if the language is relatively uncomplicated, the sentiments certainly are not. In 'Old Dalby' A wind turbine is pictured thus:

> a hissing flow of metal –
> the movement we have invented
> to not be still with our selves.

and the poem 'Crow' opens with the mesmeric lines:

> The hill stands open like a house in summer.
> And there is my soul,
> riding the ragged winds.

We read the first part of this collection with a growing sense of disquiet, aware of the poet's fear for the planet, and his doubt about our ability to care effectively for each other and ourselves. Then, there is an epiphany, a welcome transformation, that breaks through the solitary pessimism. This epiphany involves another:

All I can tell you then
is that I woke one morning
to find someone beside me

to whom I could say *Yes*
with all my being.
My one wise decision
was to hold onto that.
('Advice for Those Who Are Not Yet Fifty Years Old')

Many of the subsequent poems reveal an intense emotional shift, an idea of personal liberation, and a (tempered) hopefulness. To return to the 'plum' question, now 'there may be enough sun within' ('Before the Plum Harvest').

The final two poems embody the nature of the change. 'Song' is a poem of couplets that describes the mutative coming-together of the personal and the natural world: 'I thought the earth was a sorrow. / Also, it is a psalm.'

And the last poem, 'The End of Summer', is a lyrical, not-quite-sonnet that embodies a notion of hope, together with the presence of another, a companion on this troubling but important journey:

In teeming lanes, we gathered seeds on fabric
and fur, then doubled back to the shadowed pond,
shook off this new adornment as we strode.
We must have drawn a line across this land.
Not visible yet, but shining soon.

Clarke has written this journey, not only through seasons and fields, but also through an emotional landscape, overshadowed by an abiding anxiety about the future of our earth.

Diana Cant

Reviews in Brief

Rachel Carney
Octopus Mind
Seren, £9.99

In her debut collection, Rachel Carney shares in delightful and original ways her experiences of being diagnosed as an adult with dyspraxia and neurodivergence. In 'Nine Brains at Midnight' a battle is waged within the speaker's brain; each conflicting voice demands space: 'The first brain wallows in the ache.' while 'The seventh brain is composing a poem about a person who lies awake at midnight, composing a poem.'

As often happens, late diagnosis can come as a relief. In 'The clues were all there, strewn out along the shore' the poet hides the letters of 'dyspraxia' within the text, and she encounters 'the constant *r* of the sea'. At times Carney's humour turns more surreal, for example in 'The Test', where the speaker goes for an unspecified test (sounding like Covid) and spews out tiny corpses, 'Each one looked like a miniature version of me.'

The back cover tells us Carney has a great interest in ekphrasis. Too often ekphrastic poems do little more than describe a painting. In Carney's case her poetry leaps way beyond any frame. In 'Unremarkable', after Gwen John, the poet cleverly illustrates the drafting and editing process by using anaphora and repetition, for example, 'A woman paints a small, secluded corner of herself [...]//A woman paints a corner of her mind', and later, 'A woman paints her way from rue du Cherche-Midi to rue du Cherche-Midi [...]'.

The poet employs a wide variety of form, from villanelle to free verse. The prose poem 'Normally' parodies the poet's experience of writing: 'I'm ~~wring~~ writing the ~~wrd~~ word *n-o-r-m-a-l-l-y*, ~~bur~~ but ~~m~~ I'm tired, so ~~aough aluogh~~ although my brain has ~~alry~~ already ~~sipd~~ skipped to the next'.

Images of animals and the natural world are used, often in startling ways, to show how diagnosis has enabled the speaker to become herself. Thus, in 'Growing', she writes 'Yesterday, a small green bud/ sprouted behind my left ear', and 'I root myself in fertile earth,'.

Self-acceptance is well-captured in 'Mine': 'I've known you always/ in the small pearl of your absence// drifting slowly away from me', and in the tender 'Sorry': 'and in the end I just have to give in and let her be sorry – / this lady who has been sorry all her life,/ sorry that she doesn't understand and cannot spell'.

Heartwarming and real, I recommend this book!

David Mohan
Wildfire
Against the Grain, £6

The lyrical poems in Mohan's debut pamphlet are haunted by a sense of loss, for a lover, a mother and the world we live in. The title is sadly apposite for our times and provides both backdrop and metaphor to what is being burned to dust. The cyclical nature of dust is considered through black humour in 'Vacuum', where it becomes returned 'to the carpet,/ to mattresses, polished surfaces,/ like a mourner emptying ash.'

The book opens with the title poem, where 'The world is kindling for a dropped match,' prepares the reader for igniting moments of love and grief.

> It lived in the minds of alchemists,
> brimstone sermons, nuclear stations,
>
> riled and vicious and ready to terminate
> this touch paper planet.

The recurring motif of 'red', with its associations of fire, blood, passion, is also the colour of the speaker's mother's hair. In 'Arrangement in Red and Gold, Number One' Mohan conveys the sense of shock that accompanies death, when he writes, 'We hadn't even guessed it was death// come to visit, hadn't practised our pose.', as they stand by her bed, 'your henna hair always too bright.'

The power of an intensely shared moment can transcend years and is elegantly captured in 'The Blood Husband', where the 'three spots of blood' might lean towards fairytale, or refer to Exodus and the three drops of wine spilled at the Seder. In the poem loss is accepted as the aftermath of desire

> ... blood husband
> you wrestled with
> the previous evening
> transformed overnight

In another homo-erotic poem, 'Hotel d'Alsace' (where fellow Irish poet Oscar Wilde died), the speaker tenderly conveys the grief experienced when 'we meet like acquaintances after long absence - / two guests who know there is no easy exit...'

A stand-out poem for me was 'Evergreen Delta' evocatively describing a long-distance relationship: 'We walk on either shore, headland to headland,/ facing each other like lighthouses.'

There is much to enjoy in this pamphlet, with its many sonnets, and interweaving of repeated words (beds, hair, dust, ash, ghosts) and colours (red, black, white, gold), possibly to show that the past is ever-present and distance can disappear in a moment of meeting.

One such sizzling moment is illustrated in the evocative 'Coastal', the closing poem, presumably about a long-distance relationship: 'It is almost morning on my coast,/ on yours the night is drawing in' as the two seemingly communicate through a chat room 'skimming oceans between our talk,// as though we occupied bodies/ that kindle one electric thought'.

These are evocative, lyrical, tender poems.

Rosie Jackson
Love Leans over the Table
Two Rivers Press, £10.99

The epigraph of Jackson's latest collection shows the title comes from a 14th-century poem about a longing for the beloved.

The narrator grew up in a Christian household, where 'Prayer got Dad through most things' ('In a Cold Place'). While her mother, wanted 'a real bloke', Jackson learned 'it can take a long time/ to find our life's work – to learn what real loving is.' ('The Ground We Stand On').

In the poet's search for real loving, the beloved becomes understood as divine love. Spirituality is not an obvious thematic choice for today's secular world, yet Jackson's poems, travelling through trauma and professed atheism to serenity, are moving and grounded.

Picking out key poems is not easy, but for me one has to be 'The Day Meher Baba Died' which glides forwards and backwards, and across continents, from when, with 'satchel bulging with homework and atheism' ('Letter to Nietzsche'), the narrator first heard about this Indian spiritual master who ultimately changed her life. She writes with searing honesty in a sestina of her experiences of becoming a teenage mother ('Don't think these doors will ever close'), poignantly followed by a poem about losing a custody battle for her son ('After Reading Wendy Pratt's *When I Think of My Body as a Horse*'). The trauma this caused is captured in 'Coming to Terms With', where the same words are repeated yet rearranged in floating form, across the page, paralleling a sense of dissociation and shock. This is one of many examples of Jackson's mastery in balancing form with content.

In ‘Let’s Call it Light’, which closes the first section, Jackson describes her spiritual awakening: ‘there I was, 3am, in the same shaking,/ shocked, wondering-what-tornado-had-passed-through-me state/ as when my son was born’.

I’ve dwelt at length on the first section, as to me it underpins the book. However the other sections are packed with jewels of poems. The middle section, ‘Better than Angels’, considers many eastern and western mystics and philosophers, such as the exquisite ‘The Boisterous Sobbings of Margery Kempe’ one about Julian of Norwich, while the closing section ‘Among Mortals’ seems to return to the material world as a spiritually awakened being. One I particularly like in this section is ‘The Golden Bough’: ‘And I want to cry out, as Frigga did,// to the air and birds and new-found tenderness of the world,/ that love is surely bigger than grief, than death.’

This is a book to treasure, where grief is held in loving hands and tenderly transformed. Images of and lines from Jackson’s poems will want to stay with you.

Mark Waldron
Straight Up Giant
Bloodaxe, £12

Waldron’s fifth collection brims with metaphysical satire, and the reader may laugh uncomfortably, looking into the shadows of the world s/he inhabits. Near the start of the book is ‘How a Poem Works’: ‘it’s sticky I should have said’, the speaker writes, and it has ‘an ending that lets you down so you can step off it effortlessly// [...] changed but entirely unchanged’. This possibly both describes the writing process and carries an echo of Beckett’s *Endgame* with its themes of beginnings and endings being intertwined and existence being cyclical.

The collection starts with ‘Panic Room’ and ends with the word ‘Nothing’ (‘Bacon and Egg’), but the book doesn’t quite end there, as there is an epilogue: *‘A winter mist rose off the Hackney Marshes pitches, and the old/ sun hung still a while longer, before it moved on.’* This complements the epigraph, from the eighth-century scholar and poet, Alcuin of York, ‘Why do we love you, world, when you run away from us?/ You keep running away, and yet we still love you.’

It seems to be the cyclical and slippery nature of life that motivates Waldron, alongside his quirky humour. His ‘eleven grim poems’ open with ‘Blossom’: ‘Once there lived a brother and sister// twins called Blossom and Blossom// Blossom was cruel and kind’. One could read this as different sides of one's nature, but trying to make sense of poems is often a mistake; it is best to enter their unique world.

Untitled, italicised prose poems intersect titled poems. Written in first-person narrator they possibly offer a direct way to read the non-italicised poems: '*Are our secrets so well disguised that in showing them we hide them further?*' (p.84)

Several blank pages are also included. One example interrupts the poem 'The Piece of String' – which brought to mind a line from Jack Spicer 's poem 'A Book of Music' where 'Poetry ends like a rope' in the ocean.[2] Waldron seems to end his poem with 'a string is tied to a tree//while its other end leads into a hole in the floor', for facing this is a blank page, then another blank page. However, then the poem continues 'only to emerge once more'. As if the blank pages reflect what's not said in the poem.

For all Waldron's humour, death and nihilism are very present, and near the end of the collection the poet refers to four important deaths that occurred during the creation of the book, which is dedicated to their memory.

Finally, it is worth discovering (if you haven't already) Waldron's performance, especially his videos (including one of him in a bath[3]) : his inimitable deadpan voice will stay in your head as you read the poems.

Sarah Doyle
(m)othersongs
V. Press, £6.50

The nineteen poems in *(m)othersongs* are described on the cover as 'very meteorological and very moonlit', and readers learn Sarah Doyle is a current PhD candidate researching meteorological poetry. Combined with the poet's experiences of endometriosis and infertility, I anticipated watery, weather poems, but if there was a dominant element it was earth, particularly autumn. 'Corn Dolly' opens the pamphlet, with some stunning images, 'I am stiff-skirted, wide-/ legged, fecund and// pregnant with home-/spun magic'. This poem uses 'I am' as anaphora, a device similarly employed in 'Milker' and 'Hollowed' where this captures the emptiness of being unable to conceive: 'I am an egg devoid of yolk'.

Doyle enjoys soundplay, for example, 'slappy sandals/clip/clop/ clapping ('Near Misses') and rhyme, as in 'Milker': 'swaying my wide

[2] https://hispirits.blogspot.com/2009/02/book-of-music-by-jack-spicer.html
[3] https://www.bloodaxebooks.com/ecs/product/a-straight-up-giant-1326

arse/ soft as the damp grass', and the closing section of 'Creation Myth': '*You'd make a lovely mum*, I'm told./ But I know this is a myth: that I/ am empty, sterile, and cold.' Presumably here 'cold' signifies feeling dead, though to me the speaker comes across more as deeply unhappy. In the fifth section of this poem, the speaker's abject sadness can be felt in 'Sometimes I talk to the babies/ I could not have.'

'BLOOD CYCLE', which is in four parts, carries a byline '*In which a Disease and her Treatments speak*' and gives endometriosis a powerfully visceral voice:

> I am Goddess of Dysmenorrhoea, robed
> in crimson, shining like liver: a rust-slick
> twisting. I am thigh-streak, gut-knife
> the quiver of blood clots, jellyfish-soft.

The anguish and consuming nature of being unable to conceive can cause untold suffering: 'The moon wanted nothing more/ than to bear the sun's children;' ('Celestial'). The pressure on a relationship is captured in 'INTERLUDE', where a newlywed couple make a ragdoll from the wife's wedding dress, but in time, they tear it apart, 'each wielding their tattered share'.

One poem I found particularly moving was 'Windsong, for my mother': 'Forgive me those times I slipped my moorings: the safe harbour of your arms, your kitchen/ table counsel', summed up at the end of the poem as 'belief, courage, hope.' The poems in this pamphlet pay tribute to this counsel.

Fahad Al-Amoudi
when the flies come
ignition press, £6

A note to foreground this debut pamphlet describes how Prince Alemayehu, only son of Emperor Tewodros II, was taken to England in 1868 following his father's suicide (after losing the Battle of Maqdala to the British) and his mother's death. The lonely young prince was forbidden from communicating with his former homeland and died, from pleurisy, before he turned nineteen.

Six poems in the pamphlet are imagined letters from Alemayehu. These are interspersed with the poet's personal reflections on family and place. I'd be interested in the poetic choice not to group the Alemayehu poems together, as at times it disrupted my reading, but perhaps it was to show that the past is felt in the present.

The poet's roots are in Ethiopia and Yemen, but revisiting a homeland sometimes gives a view through different eyes: in the first of the 'personal' poems, 'Amateur Bug Catcher,' the narrator travels to Menagesha in Western Ethiopia: 'Walking up this road, young boys look at me/ as if recognising a dead explorer [...] open their hands//like this place is a mistranslation of flower,'.

There are many dazzling lines. In '*Unsorted Extracts of Letters [1874-76]*', the speaker, describing autumn, writes, 'The sky is a paper bag, flecked with leaves the colour of a looted city.'; in '*iii Unsent [circa. 1878]*', 'You said I was a library,/ quiet and sun-spotted, a leopard/ sleeping in a tree.' The book is dedicated to the poet's late mother, and in 'Mum's Jewellery', 'pearls crowd her neck like evening/ around a church spire;' while in 'Tarmac', 'We were there to say goodbye. The word goodbye was never said.'

Death haunts these poems: that of the young prince and his parents, of the poet's mother, and others. And there are flies, not just in the title, but in several poems. Attracted to decomposing matter, their presence can symbolise transformation, perseverance and bravery. 'If your body is a fly, caught/ in Ethiopian opal// I am your refraction.' ('*vi The Black Epistle [letter to Alemayehu]*').

The poet employs a wide variety of form, and the pamphlet ends with the prose poem 'Grave Robin' wherein the speaker, tending the grave of his mother, notices a robin watching: 'together we steal whatever light there is left in the day, our voices finding, at last, one harmony.' Here is a pamphlet you're likely to feel enriched for having read.

Mary Mulholland

Acknowledgements

Contributors

Patrick Agnew lives just outside Lismore in Waterford, Ireland. He completed a full time MA in Creative Writing with the Department of English in UCC in 2020. He spends his spare time writing, reading, listening, cycling and working away in the garden.

Vasiliki Albedo's poems have appeared in *Poetry Review, Poetry London, Wasafiri, Oxford Poetry* and elsewhere. She won Poetry International's chapbook competition and the Poetry Society's 2022 Stanza competition, jointly, Live Canon's pamphlet competition and was commended in the National Poetry competition.

Julian Bishop's first collection of eco poems, called *We Saw It All Happen,* was published earlier this year by Fly On The Wall Press. He's currently working on a collection of poems about the life and times of the Italian painter Caravaggio.

Penny Blackburn lives in North-East England and has appeared in a wide variety of publications, including online in *Atrium, Riggwelter* and *Phare* and in print with *Dream Catcher, Lighthouse* and *Spelt.* Her collection with Yaffle is due Autumn 2023. She is on Twitter and Facebook as @penbee8.

Carole Bromley is a York-based poet. Three collections with Smith|Doorstop and one with Valley Press. Winner of a number of prizes, including the Bridport and the Hamish Canham Award as well as the 2022 Caterpillar Prize for poems for children.

Nia Broomhall has just completed an MA in Creative Writing. Head of English at a comprehensive school, she has been teaching for 22 years. She was Highly Commended in the Winchester Poetry Prize 2022 and has been longlisted again this year. She has been published by *Magma, Dreich* and others.

Roger Camp is the author of three photography books including the award winning *Butterflies in Flight*, Thames & Hudson, 2002 and *Heat*, Charta, Milano, 2008. His documentary photography has been awarded Europe's prestigious Leica Medal of Excellence. Represented by the Robin Rice Gallery, NYC, more of his work may be seen on Luminous-Lint.com.

Diana Cant is a poet and child psychotherapist. Her poems have been published in various anthologies and magazines, including *Agenda*, *The North* and *Poetry News*. Her most recent pamphlet, *At Risk – the lives some children live*, was published by Dempsey and Windle in 2021. This year she's been nominated for the Forward Prize for best individual poem and also won the Plaza Poetry Prize.

Deb Catesby is a writer and artist living near Herefordshire. Previously a playwright, since 2020 she has been seduced by poetry. Her poems have been published in the *The Alchemy Spoon* and twice longlisted for the Fish prize. Her painting, 'Family Dinner', was shortlisted for the 2023 Royal Academy summer show.

Jo Colley is a writer, poet and film maker who lives in Darlington. Her latest poetry collection, *Sleeper*, was published by Smokestack in 2020. Her work has appeared in many magazines. She has won prizes for poetry films, short stories and flash fiction and runs Blueprint, a poetry press.

Alexandra Corrin-Tachibana is author of *Sing me down from the dark* (SALT, 2022). She was shortlisted for the Fish Prize, Leeds Poetry Festival Award and the Winchester Poetry Prize in 2023 . She is published in *PN Review*, *The North*, *Poetry Wales*, *Artemis* and *The Moth*. She teaches at The Writing School and has MAs in Writing Poetry and in Japanese culture.

Jasper Deane is a London based artist who, since graduating from the RCA in 1978, has exhibited works in various media, in London and abroad. He has recently been described as 'a London creative' having contributed to many and various creative projects over the years. He paints in oil and watercolour and also makes artists books.

Alice Eaves is an artist and writer from Blackpool, England. She is a runner-up for the Grierson Verse Prize, recipient of a Peshkar Artist Development Award and Curator of the Ukraine Writers Project. She holds an MSc in Creative Writing from the University of Edinburgh.

Duncan Forbes's poems have been published by Faber, Secker and Enitharmon, who brought out a Selected Poems in 2009, drawn from five previous collections. For his most recent collection of poems, *Human Time* (2020), see www.duncanforbes.com. He read English and has taught for many years.

Lara Frankena lives in London. Her poems have appeared in publications such as *Magma, Oxford Poetry* and *Poetry News* and were longlisted for the 2021, 2022 and 2023 Erbacce Prize.

SK Grout (she/they) is an editor and writer who grew up in Aotearoa New Zealand, lived in Germany, and now splits her time between London and Auckland Tamaki Makaurau. Her debut chapbook is *What love would smell like* (V.Press, 2021). https://skgroutpoetry.wixsite.com/poetry

Tamsin Hopkins writes poetry and fiction. She has an MA in Creative Writing from Royal Holloway and is a previous winner of The Aesthetica Prize. Poems have appeared in *Mslexia, The London Magazine, Magma,* and *The Alchemy Spoon*. Her pamphlet *Inside the Smile* is published by Cinnamon Press.

Julie Irigaray is the author of the poetry pamphlet *Whalers, Witches and Gauchos* (Nine Pens, 2021). Her poems appeared internationally in *The Rialto*, *Magma*, *Ambit*, and *Poetry Wales*. She was commended in the 2020 Ambit Magazine Poetry Prize and selected as one of the *Best New British and Irish Poets 2018*.

Ian Irwin is a Bristol-based writer and educator. He is an Out-Spoken Press Emerging Poet and has poems published in *Trasna* and *Poetry Pulpit Anthology*.

Maria Isakova Bennett from Liverpool creates the poetry journal Coast to Coast to Coast. Awarded a Peggy Poole Award by Vona Groarke, a New North Poet Award by Clare Pollard, Maria was awarded the Teignmouth Poetry Prize by Fiona Benson this year. Maria has a fifth pamphlet forthcoming from Hazel Press.

Dillon Jaxx is a queer disabled writer living in Sussex, working on their first collection. Published in print and online including *Poetry Wales* and *Ink, Sweat & Tears*. Winner of the Rebecca Swift Writing Prize 2022.

L B Jørgensen lives in Denmark where she does translation and subtitling work when not trying her hand at poetry. She has had poems published in several magazines and had a poem nominated for the Pushcart Prize in 2022.

Fiona Larkin's debut collection, *Rope of Sand*, was published by Pindrop Press in 2023. Her pamphlets are *Vital Capacity* (Broken Sleep, 2022) and *A Dovetail of Breath* (Rack Press, 2020). Highly commended in the Forward Prizes, she manages innovative projects with Corrupted Poetry.

Jane Lovell's work focuses on our relationship with the planet and its wildlife, She recently won the Ginkgo Prize and Rialto/RSPB Nature & Place Competition. Her latest collection, *On Earth, as it is,* has just been published by Hazel Press.

Louise Lovell lives and works in Padua, Italy. She graduated from Brighton University in Graphic Design and has a PGCE from Goldsmiths' College, London. She has spent many years teaching art at the English International School of Padua and also working as a freelance artist on a variety of commissions from murals, restoration and illustrations.

Dave Martin, poet and historian, has published in *Dreich, Nutmeg, Orbis, South, The New European, The Poetry Village* and *Torquay United F C football programmes*. He has published two chapbooks *Come On You Yellow's* and *A pack of tricks we play upon the dead.*

Aoife Mannix is the author of a novel, four collections of poetry, two pamphlets and six libretti. She has worked as a script editor for the BBC as well as for Channel 4 and the Royal Court Theatre. She has a PhD in creative writing from Goldsmiths, University of London.

Abegail Morley is one of the co-editors of Against the Grain Press, an innovative small independent poetry publisher. She is a Nine Arches Press poet with *The Unmapped Woman* and *The Skin Diary*. Her debut, *How to Pour Madness into a Teacup,* was shortlisted for The Forward Prize Best First Collection.

Cheryl Moskowitz is a poet, novelist and creative translator. She facilitates writing projects in community settings including schools, prisons, refugee centres, and with the homeless. She is an editor at *Magma* and co-founder of the poetry and electronic series, *All Saints Sessions* www.allsaintssessions.uk

Sarah Mnatzaganian is an Anglo-Armenian poet. Her debut, *Philosophy Revision*, published by Against the Grain Poetry Press won the 2022 Saboteur Award. Poems have featured in *PN Review, The Rialto, Poetry Wales, Poetry Ireland Review, Salzburg Review, The North, Magma, Poetry News, Poetry in the Waiting Room* and numerous anthologies.

Benedict Newbery's poems have appeared in *Ambit, Magma, The North, Finished Creatures, Borderlines, Other Poetry* and *The Morning Star*. Magma board member and production manager (2017-2020) – and lead editor for *Magma 74*. Awarded three METAL residencies. He makes poetry films: The Royal Oak was commissioned for C4's Random Acts.

Frances Rose O'Leary lives and writes in London where she works in politics, communications and the bourbon industry. She has been published in *Well Versed,* longlisted twice for the National Poetry Competition and has read poetry at events and festivals in London and New York.

Kathryn Pallant is a British-Australian writer. Her poems have appeared in *PN Review, Under the Radar, Antiphon, The Moth* and elsewhere. She has a PhD in creative writing from the University of Manchester and has taught at Lancaster University and the University of Manchester.

Stephen Payne was born in Merthyr Tydfil and lives in Penarth, South Glamorgan. He has published two full collections with HappenStance Press, and, most recently, a pamphlet, *The Wax Argument & Other Thought Experiments'*. He is Professor Emeritus at the University of Bath.

Fiona Perry began writing seriously in her early forties. Her first collection of poetry, *Alchemy* (Turas Press, Dublin), won the Poetry Book Awards (2021) Silver Medal and was shortlisted for the Rubery Prize. Her flash fiction, *Sea Change*, won first prize in the Bath Flash Fiction Awards (2020).

D A Prince lives in Leicestershire and London. Her second collection (*Common Ground*, HappenStance, 2014) won the East Midlands Book Award 2015. Her third collection, *The Bigger Picture* (also from HappenStance) was published in 2022.

Sultana Raza has exhibited in Europe (Art Monaco, ECA-EU) and the USA (Art Expo, NY). Her art-works will/have appeared in *Bewildering Stories*, *Amon Hen & Vingilot* (Tolkien Society) as Cover Art in *Focus* (BSFA, 2022 & 2023), *3Elements Review* ((inside: 2016, 2022), cover: 2023), and *Rigorous* (2023).

Julie Runacres is recently retired and based in Leicestershire, having taught English Literature and creative writing at schools in Oxford and West London. Longlisted in the 2022 National Poetry Competition, her poems have appeared in journals in the UK and the US. She is a member of the Crocodile Collective.

Lesley Sharpe teaches literature and creative writing, and her poems, reviews and essays have been published in several journals and anthologies. Her work has also been short and longlisted for a number of prizes. She co-founded Lodestone Poets with Dave Wakely and Sarala Estruch, and is also a member of Red Door Poets.

Jeff Skinner's poems have been published in competition anthologies and in journals including *Poetry Salzburg, Fenland Poetry Journal, Orbis, South,* and *Acumen.* He received a 'special mention' in this year's Coast to Coast to Coast competition.

Kris Spencer has work published in journals in the UK, US, Eire, Europe, Australia, India and SE Asia. His debut collection, *Life Drawing*, was published in 2022 by Kelsay Books. His second collection, *Contact Sheets*, is due for publication early 2024, also by Kelsay Books.

Elle Stear works as a tutor and part time librarian and uses her creativity to design worksheets and resources for students. Her work has appeared in a public story trail for an arts festival. Her writing is inspired by art, nature, folklore and loss. She has recently completed an M.A. in creative writing.

Paul Stephenson has three pamphlets: *Those People* (Smith|Doorstop, 2015), *The Days that Followed Paris* (HappenStance, 2016), written after the November 2015 terrorist attacks; and *Selfie with Waterlilies* (Paper Swans Press, 2017). He helps curate Poetry in Aldeburgh. His debut collection *Hard Drive* was published by Carcanet in summer 2023.

Lauren Thomas is a Welsh writer living in Hertfordshire. She has been published in various print and online publications including, *Magma, Lighthouse Journal, Nine Pens, the New Welsh Review* and *The London Magazine*. She has an MA in poetry writing at Newcastle University, with Poetry School London.

Oenone Thomas is a poet, psychotherapist and chocolatemaker. She is in her second Writing Poetry MA year at Poetry School, London. She was brought up in South Wales and southern Spain and now lives in the south of England.

Anthony Tomkins is a researcher at the University of York, working on addiction narratives. He writes about the hills and plains of his Brecon Beacons home and other magical things. He is an enthusiastically average runner, and his poetry can be read in *Amethyst Review, Dreich* and *Carmen Et Error*.

Mark Waldron has published five poetry collections, most recently, *A Straight Up Giant* with Bloodaxe Books in 2023. He's been published widely in magazines in the UK and the US, and his work has been translated into Spanish, Romanian and Serbian.

Sue Wallace-Shaddad has an MA in Poetry from Newcastle University. Her latest book, *Sleeping Under Clouds,* a collaboration with artist Sula Rubens, was published by Clayhanger Press, April 2023. Dempsey & Windle published her pamphlet *A City Waking Up* (2020). Sue is Secretary of Suffolk Poetry Society. suewallaceshaddad.wordpress.com

Submission Guidelines

We welcome submissions of up to three brilliant, unpublished, original poems on the issue's theme through the website during the submission window. You will find full details of how to submit on our website: www.alchemyspoon.org.

We are only able to accept submissions from those over 18.

If you have poems published in the current issue of *The Alchemy Spoon*, then we ask that you wait out one issue before submitting more work.

Simultaneous submissions are permitted but please tell us straightaway if a poem is accepted for publication elsewhere.

We aim for a speedy turnaround and will respond to every submission, but we don't offer individual feedback.

Authors retain all rights. However, if a poem is then published elsewhere, please acknowledge that it first appeared in *The Alchemy Spoon.*

Our submission window for Issue 12 will be open 1 – 29 February 2024, the theme for the issue will be 'Elements' and we will welcome poems on this theme up to 40 lines. See our website for full details.

Submission Guidelines for Essays
If you have an essay on some cutting-edge poetry-related topic, please send it to us during the submission window for consideration +/- 1500 words.

Submission Guidelines for Artwork
We are always looking for original artwork to feature on future magazine covers. Portrait-orientated images work best (or images suitable for cropping). Good quality lower resolution images can be sent at the submission stage, but higher res files will be needed (2480 pixels x 3508 pixels) at print stage. Please email us with your images as an attachment.

Submission Guidelines for Reviews
If you would like to recommend a poetry collection or submit a review of a collection, then please email us or use the contact form on the website.

Poetry Workshops
The Alchemy Spoon editors offer a one-to-one poetry feedback and workshopping service without prejudice via Zoom or Facetime. All profits from this contribute to the cost of running Clayhanger Press. Please email requests for feedback to: vanessa.tas@btinternet.com to arrange this.

News and Notes

The Alchemy Spoon position on material produced using Artificial Intelligence (AI)

The editors will not knowingly use AI artworks for magazine covers or illustrations.

We will continue to support human artists and designers and work towards a position where we are able to pay for artwork that we use.

Our submission system will be updated to reflect this position.
The editors will not knowingly accept and publish AI generated or assisted poems, reviews or articles.

We reserve the right to reject any submission that we suspect to be primarily generated or created by AI software.

As part of the submission process all submitters will be required to confirm that AI has not been used to create the work.

Could you be a guest editor for a future issue?

We have had a great time working with our guest editors and have decided to make this a more regular event for some future issues.

As guest editor you will take part in the selection of poems for the issue, take a major role in curating the order and position of the selected poems, write the editorial, and introduce 'your' issue at the Live Zoom Launch.

We are looking for people with a love of poetry and a flair for creating a well-produced final product within the agreed time frame.

If you think you would like the opportunity of being a guest editor of *The Alchemy Spoon* then email us with one side of A4 containing a short CV and the reasons why you think you will be suitable for this position

Email your application to alchemyspoon@btinternet.com

Cover Design by Clayhanger Press

Typesetting and Design Roger Bloor
Senior Copy Editor Sara Levy
Proof-reader Adam Lampert

www.clayhangerpress.co.uk

Clayhanger Press

Printed in Great Britain
by Amazon

32266430R00066